RATIONAL POLEMICS

TACKLING THE ETHICAL DILEMMAS OF LIFE

Richard Todd Devens

outskirtspress

DENVER, COLORADO

Outskirts Press, Inc.
http://www.outskirtspress.com

ISBN: 978-1-4327-9880-2

Library of Congress Control Number: 2012923395

Outskirts Press and the "OP" logo are trademarks belonging to Outskirts Press, Inc.

PRINTED IN THE UNITED STATES OF AMERICA

To my dad, Joseph Devens, who always believed in me

Table of Contents

Preface

The genesis of this book can be traced to my long-standing disillusionment with religion. I was born Jewish, and considered myself to be a Jew throughout my young years. But the older I got, the more I started to suspect that the things I was told, and things which were considered to be doctrine, just didn't make sense. I was told that being a "good" person added years to one's life. But then I kept observing good people who died before their time — from natural causes, and in tragedies, or those killed by bad people who were never caught. When I observed bad people who lived long lives, I realized that something didn't add up. I will give many examples of things I have heard that similarly "did not add up."

It is not "cool" to be an atheist. We are greatly outnumbered, and without knowing anything else about us, many of our "believing" counterparts instantly feel morally superior. God-fearing believers, it seems, have a monopoly on righteousness. At times, I would try to bring up the topic with my mother, but didn't get very far. "The smartest people in the world believe in God," she said. She was right, but intelligence and rationality are not automatically synonymous. Similarly, smart people do *very* stupid things.

Many years after I completely repudiated the idea of religion or a supreme being, I heard the late brilliant comedian George Carlin's take on religion, *Religion Is Bullshit*. How I wish I could have had the opportunity to hear him live, meet him, and shake his hand. In a small way, his act bothered me, but not on account of the content. Here was someone who was saying things that I had believed for years, and it was almost as if he were taking the words right out of my mouth. It's funny; when a famous author or comedian says something, it lends an air of legitimacy to it. So perhaps I'm not a total crackpot...or at least, not the *only* one.

Although I had originally conceived this to be a book dealing with the concept of God and religion, my thoughts branched out into various offshoots. I thought about trying to come up with answers to questions such as: What constitutes morality? What is evil? How do we deal with evil people? Is the death penalty intrinsically unjust? Is vigilante justice ever justified when we have exhausted all other options? Why is it okay to kill small animals, but not bad people? What constitutes "a higher form of life"? These are some of the topics I address, although I go off into some tangential ones, as well. After all, religion is supposed to be the arbiter of what constitutes "good" or moral behavior. But religious people don't always act in "good" or moral ways.

I will have some harsh things to say about religion and the hypocrisies surrounding it. But let me be clear: I *truly* respect a person's right to believe in, and to practice, any religion he wishes, as long as it does not interfere with the rights of others. Proselytizing is not intrinsically wrong; proselytizers believe so strongly in their faith that they want others to, as well. They want them to "see the light." But when it is done against someone's will, especially by force, then it is wrong. A religious Palestinian, Taliban, al-Qaeda, or Muslim terrorist is an oxymoron.

Just because I may not believe what someone else believes, that does not mean I cannot comprehend how important their religion is to them, how much it uplifts them, offers them hope, and comforts them in times of grief and sorrow. When I hear about the desecration of a house of worship, I am mortified. It is truly sacrilegious; it is blasphemy.

I once saw a segment on the news about a Torah which was desecrated at a synagogue. The congregation was grief-stricken and held a funeral for it. I did not have to follow the Torah to appreciate its significance to the Jewish people. The desecration of a house of worship or a Torah is criminal, and the perpetrators should be prosecuted to the fullest extent of the law.

I have always marveled at the architecture, the beauty, and the majesty of churches. I want to visit the famous churches around the world that I have not yet seen, as I consider them to be historical and cultural institutions. I applaud all the time and effort that went into their creation, even if I don't share the beliefs of the people who constructed them. All that is important is what *they* believed, and I admire them for wanting to represent their beliefs and to congregate in such monumental structures.

When I thought of a title for my book, the word "polemics" came to mind. *Random House Webster's College Dictionary* defines polemics as: 1. the art or practice of disputation or controversy. 2. the branch of theology dealing with ecclesiastical disputation and controversy.

The second definition is not applicable to my book, but the first one definitely is. Because I, nevertheless, consider my arguments to be rational, *Rational Polemics* seemed like the perfect title. I thought it also had a great *ring* to it. I then Googled the title, and immediately, *The Rational Polemicist* came up. It is "a website and blog devoted to examining the most controversial, ethical, social, and political issues from a rational point of view." Their definitions of polemics are: "of or involving dispute or controversy; an argument of controversy, esp. over doctrines, beliefs, [or] ideologies." My knee-jerk reaction was "Shit!"

In addition to *The Rational Polemicist*, there was a listing: *Rational Polemics about UFOs and the ET Hypothesis.*

Not *ever* wanting to plagiarize — even inadvertently — I was prepared to choose another title. But as an afterthought, I mentioned this to an author adviser at Outskirts Press, who told me that titles are not copyrighted. This is why I chose to leave the title as-is.

There are people who will consider what I have written to be outrageous. There are people who will "know" I am wrong. This is okay. Healthy, peaceful, and *rational* debate is always welcome. I feel very strongly about what I have written, and have a right to express my views...as you do.

Sometimes I have used the masculine pronoun *he* instead of *he and she*. This was solely for purposes of convenience. In the chapter "The Rude Brood," I sometimes refer to *waitresses*, and sometimes to *waiters*. When I referred to the former, *waitresses and waiters* would have been equally applicable.

I would be remiss if I didn't include a word about my brother, Scott Devens. Computer skills are not my strong point, to say the least (especially when dealing with a sick — and slow — computer). He guided me through all kinds of obstacles that came up along the way (including a time of horror when I thought several pages, and many hours, of work were permanently erased). I could not have completed the book without his help.

Thanks also to my cousin, Martin Davidowitz, who skillfully and patiently helped me through various computer functions that I could never have performed on my own.

A special thank you is in order for my amazing editor Joan Rogers, whose help and input were more than I could ever have hoped for.

CHAPTER 1

Religion:
The Universal Farce

No other concept has been shrouded in such mystery as the existence of God. To the devout believers, the way He works and His justifications for allowing certain events to take place might be deemed mysterious, but not His existence per se. To these devout believers, His existence is factual, an irreducible primary. Some have questioned His existence because they have not received evidence through their senses. They are often told by believers that the very fact that they do not feel His existence indicates a deficiency in *them*. They are not allowing themselves to accept God, to let Him into their lives. "First you must believe," they are told. "Then you will feel God's presence."

I do not believe in God; even before my views became crystallized, I continuously witnessed hypocrisies in the name of religion. After tragedies, I heard the same nonsense repeated over and over again. These statements became so common that they were never questioned. As a result, they were accepted as the correct, not to mention the *proper* thing to say. In my mind, I am an atheist. But because I would never purport to know the unknowable, my stating that there is no God would make me as guilty as those who state — on faith — that there *is* one. Because of this distinction, some would say I am an agnostic. Not one for classifications or titles, suffice it to say I will believe in God when I am given proof enough to satisfy me. I will never put the cart before the horse and play the game of believers, who claim that belief must come first. If He does exist, the proof would have to be so self-evident that I would not have to accept it on faith. In his act *Religion Is Bullshit*, George Carlin said, "If I can see something, it kind of adds to the credibility."

To believers, the facts that the universe, Earth, and the intricacies that comprise life exist, indicate that a supreme being (usually referred to as God) exists. They point to sundry examples of the complexity of living things — human beings being the most complex. When we are hot, we sweat. Sweat is nature's air conditioner; the body knows when it is hot, and our natural cooling system kicks in involuntarily. Eyelashes are to keep dust particles out of our eyes. Our heart, lungs, capillaries, blood vessels, etc. are marvels of anatomical engineering and science, the brain being the most complex of all. In fact, no computer can approximate the complexity and ingenuity of the human brain.

In addition to our intellectual capacities, our emotional capacities are no less fascinating. Complex changes take place in the body when we are under extreme emotional stress. We cry when we feel grief, and the tears that flow from our eyes are like a stream breaking through the barriers of the dam that encloses it; when we can no longer hold in our sadness or grief, there must be a physical release. The release is deemed healthy, for it is a catharsis — a cleansing of the soul. The soul must be cleansed before it can be healed. An orgasm is a pleasurable overflowing of the dam; when combined with love, it is one of the miracles of life. Anger is a complex emotion. What takes place inside the mind of a normally sane person that makes him become insane and kill someone? What is love? Most people would have trouble defining it — or would have different definitions of it — but we know it when we feel it. And there are different kinds of love; the love for our parents is a different kind of love from the romantic love we feel for a girlfriend or boyfriend or a spouse.

The animal kingdom is a marvel of complexity too, but not quite to the extent that humans are. This, plus the fact that we are, on the whole, more intelligent, is why we are usually referred to as a "higher form of life." But observe the birds. The fact that they can fly is another marvel of natural engineering; bats being able to navigate by bouncing sound waves off objects, even though they are blind, is another example. Chipmunks can scale trees at 90-degree angles; dogs can hear frequencies that we cannot. They also have a much more acute sense of smell, and have worked wonders for law enforcement. Some birds can swoop down from great distances, with pinpoint accuracy, to get to a fish in the ocean when it is dinner time. All mothers and babies — human or animal — instinctively know how to breast-feed their young. And the babies instinctively know who their mother is, and where to get their milk. The animal kingdom is given a biological head start in their quest for survival: Skunks emit a terrible odor; other creatures are camouflaged by their color to blend in, almost undetectably, with their environment; some animals burrow holes to hide underground; weaker animals get away from stronger ones by being faster.

The above examples are but a few of the many which are cited by believers as proof of the existence of God. As to when a specific feature of the anatomy of an animal serves a specific purpose in aiding its survival, how could such marvels of nature exist, if not for the presence of a higher being? How could the trees that grow, the mountains, the oceans, and any number of these phenomena exist? "Just observe nature, the animal kingdom, and people," believers say. "That is your proof. How else could this have happened?"

But what appears to be proof to believers is not proof at all; they are merely using their own suppositions as definitions of what should indicate a higher being. And if they're asked who created God (Wouldn't an even greater power have to have created *Him*?),[1] they claim that nothing could have created God, for He always existed. Thus, they conveniently state the unknowable as an axiom in order to counter the above argument. But knowledge requires proof in the form of evidence from our senses. We may view certain things as evidence, and we may strongly believe something, but that does not make it a reality.

Many people are convinced beyond any doubt of the existence of God. If this belief enriches their lives, gives them peace of mind, hope, and comfort; if it compels them to try to be a good person who does good deeds and lives like a "religious" person should, then this belief is serving a positive purpose. They are said to have *faith,* which is belief in the absence of proof. But this does not make the existence of God a fact. He either exists, or He does not.

Many devout believers who consider the existence of God a self-evident fact obviously cannot prove this to a non-believer. So they resort to the same logic as the people (themselves included) who claim God always existed. Anyone who does not believe has to have a major deficiency. They are not open to His existence; they have not allowed Him to enter into their lives. And then they ask you to be illogical by claiming that you must believe first, and then you will see the light. In other words, you must ignore all the non-evidence, disown your own doubts, and believe something on blind faith. If you refuse to go along with it, you have the added guilt of being a sinner who is going to go to Hell for not being able to give up your mind (which God would have given you) and your better judgment.

Believers always try to set a trap for non-believers. "Why don't you believe?" they ask, when the proper question should come from *us*: "Why do you believe?" Ayn Rand has said that you shouldn't ask someone to prove a negative.

Even though there is no way of ever knowing this, let us, for argument's sake, assume that God always existed. How did this come about? Was it by an accident of fate or chance, analogous to the supposition that if two people did not happen to have sex at a particular time, a particular person would never have existed? Is His existence an accident of fate in the same manner by which some life forms ended up as people, some as dogs, ants, cockroaches, etc.? Let us also assume that God exists and is indeed an omniscient, omnipotent, and all-good supreme being. Why does this necessitate that we must love Him, even if He created us? Might we have not done likewise, if *we* were God?

Why does the existence of God necessitate that we worship and pray to Him daily, and to shower Him with praise lest He forget? Is this really done out of love, or out of fear or obligation? Is it to rack up points on Earth to keep us out of Hell when we die? Does it serve the dual function of allowing us to murder, steal, rape, hurt, and inflict pain on others, but atone for our sins? Who will accumulate the greater amount of points, the non-believer who always tries to treat others the way he likes to be treated, or the embezzler and murderer who prays in church regularly? Indeed, to call oneself a "God-fearing" man is like bestowing a badge of honor. But doesn't this fear indicate our impotence in the face of an all-powerful entity that can punish us at will for any sins — intentional or not — that we may commit? What does this really say about an entity that can engender fear in a weaker entity?[2]

I remember studying for my bar mitzvah, and being scolded for phonetically pronouncing the Hebrew word for God. I was told that one was not supposed to do that, and I remember being full of guilt and fear that I would get a sin. Similarly, I once ate cornbread on Passover, and likewise suffered the fear that I would get a sin. I did not realize until I was much older that if I were to receive a sin from God for doing something unintentionally, or doing something that I did not know was wrong, God could not be as good as He was cracked up to be.

What's even worse is the concept of "original sin." This monstrous concept is even more frightening, because it states that we are sinners simply due to the fact that we are human and not perfect. In other words, a newborn infant who has not yet learned how to think, reason, and understand language and concepts, and who has not yet learned how to hate and steal, is already a sinner just by virtue of the fact that he was born.

The contradictions and hypocrisies related to God are many. Some statements are so blatantly contradictory, but repeated so often, that they have become accepted as truth. As a child, I was told that if one were a good person, God would increase his years on Earth. This statement is so obviously false that no examples even have to be cited of truly good and productive people whose lives were snuffed out so senselessly and so early, or who otherwise died prematurely, while many of their villainous counterparts lived long lives. And what of the sinner who dies in a plane crash — because it was his time to go — while the saint sitting next to him dies too, because he happened to be in the same plane?

When one is suffering from a serious illness and seemingly recovers miraculously, escapes from a burning building, or walks away from a serious car accident with a few scratches, God is praised for saving these people. "Thank God," their relatives and friends say. "God was watching over you." In other words, God intervened. I would want to know why, if God saved these people from death, He did not prevent them from getting ill, prevent the building from burning or the person from being in it, and prevent the car crash in the first place. But assuming He intervened, and was praised for doing so, why is He not criticized when people — especially good people — die in the above situations? God does not interfere in events, I was told. But the same people will say "Thank God" when something good happens.

Another common cliché heard so often that it has become the knee-jerk response to utter after a tragedy is "Our thoughts and prayers are with the victims." I have often asked myself, "What does this mean?" The person is already dead. Wouldn't the prayers have been more beneficial *before* this person was brutally murdered?

Sometimes we know in advance that someone is in trouble. They have a life-threatening illness, or they have been kidnapped by terrorists threatening to behead him if their demands are not met. Loved ones and religious people pray for them; the person with the serious illness recovers, and the person held hostage is set free. God is praised for watching over these people. What if there were no people to pray for them? Would that have made a difference?

What about the argument that God does not interfere in these matters? Perhaps He is waiting until death to hand out people's rewards and punishments in Heaven or Hell. If the people in the above example die, however, God is not blamed. He either does not interfere in human events, or He is taking or allowing a certain person to come into Heaven early. But loved ones still grieve and mourn, even though this was "God's will," and even though "God is watching over, and has a plan for, all of us." When the person was in peril, they prayed he would live; now they pray for his soul. If some things seem too unjust and don't make any sense...well, "God works in mysterious ways," "God has a reason for everything," and "It is not right for us mortals to question the will of the Almighty." And if God has a reason for everything, and will not interfere in events, it follows that prayer will not alter an occurrence. And if it did, would we not be interfering with the will of God, with God's plan for us?

The unspeakable tragedy that occurred on September 11, 2001 brought forth some of the most asinine statements imaginable. Some people who were in the Twin Towers when the planes hit managed to get out before the buildings fell. One such person described how he crawled on his hands and knees through the darkness until he managed to find a way out. "How do you think you found your way out?" he was asked. "God showed me the way," was the answer. This statement, of course, would never be challenged, because it is the right thing to say. And because the overwhelming majority of people believe in God, it is comforting for them to think that God had a hand in saving this individual. But my question is: "Why did He not save the *other* innocent people who were murdered?" Is it possible that this individual was more "good" than all the others who perished? I challenge anyone to satisfactorily answer this question. The best I would get is: "We are not supposed to question the will of God," "The Lord works in mysterious ways," or "God was calling these people to Heaven with Him." If the latter were true, why would we pray for the safe evacuation of the people when they were first in trouble, or before they perished or we discovered that they perished? Again, would we not be interfering with the will of God?

Whether or not God exists, has a plan for all of us, or interferes in such events, it is perfectly human and natural for all decent people to be horrified by such occurrences, and to wish for the safety of their loved ones, as well as for all innocent people (even if we, as mere mortals, do not have the mental capacity or wisdom to understand the reasons why a supreme being does or does not do certain things). If God does not interfere with occurrences or the actions of even the most evil among us, how do we reconcile the events of 9/11 with the belief that it was "someone's time to go"? That would be saying that God *caused* 9/11. If He had *prevented* 9/11 from happening, how would He have been able to bring those people to Heaven whose time it was to go? Could there have been other ways for the people to have died?

If God saved some of the people who survived, that means He *interfered*. And if He interfered, it then follows that He could have *averted* 9/11 from happening in the first place. (This statement would be blasphemous to a religious person, and certainly — if there were a God — I could never conceive of Him being a "good" God if He, in fact, caused this. But if He did not cause this, how else would God have ended the life of the person whose time it was to go?)

What of the other people who perished? Was it their time to go as well, in the same manner? And if God metes out punishment only after life, and does not interfere in events and occurrences *in* life, then why would He selectively save some people and not others? Why would He heal some people, and not others? Why would He not, in His supposed infinite goodness, devise a more peaceful and less painful way to die? On that horrible day, the people in the planes, as well as the people in the Twin Towers, not only died brutal deaths, but *knew* they were going to die. For those of us who have never gone through an experience such as this, we can only *imagine* the depth of the suffering. Now...if the idea of God causing a calamity is preposterous, why is He given credit for aborting one?

People die due to hurricanes, tornadoes, tsunamis, mud slides, forest fires, floods, volcanic eruptions, and avalanches. In these cases, the cause of death is not deemed to be evil. Many people do not view natural occurrences as evil. They say that it is just nature, this is the way nature works, and one cannot pass moral judgment on it. It is what it is. They would even argue that if one knows they are living in a high-risk area (such as living on a fault line of a major earthquake zone), that they are willingly choosing to live there despite the added risk. If the earthquake *does* occur, they can't blame nature (or God)... notwithstanding the fact that an infant has no say in his domicile.

In the animal kingdom, animals eat other animals in order to survive. It is not deemed evil—except, perhaps, by the animal that is being eaten. But doomed animals *do* suffer. The mouse that is caught by a snake *knows* he is going to die. In "The Great Migration," Scott Pelley's story about the East African wildebeest migration featured on *60 Minutes* (December 2010), wildebeest (a type of African antelope) migrate 350 miles from Serengeti National Park in Tanzania to the Masai Mara reserve in Kenya (and back again). During the migration, a crocodile-infested stream had to be crossed. Some made it across. One, who was not so lucky, had his head engulfed by the jaws of a crocodile, and was summarily pushed under the water — with the help of other crocodiles — to be drowned and then eaten. I really felt for that poor wildebeest.

Species have their own built-in survival mechanisms; some animals can camouflage themselves to match their surroundings. Skunks emit a terrible odor as a defense. Others can burrow into holes in the earth. The animal kingdom represents a constant game of cat and mouse. One animal is hungry; one wants to live. And the animals who are hunted by other animals are often hunters *themselves*. But the examples of natural disasters and of the animal kingdom are not considered evil. The former is considered just a manifestation of how nature works; the latter is considered to be a kind of subset of nature. Animals — by eating other animals — are not considered to be "bad" or "immoral," but are merely acting to survive in a way consistent with their nature. 9/11, however, is an example of choice: the willful and deliberate murder of innocent people by pure evil.

Additional asinine statements are uttered by athletes when asked by interviewers what made the difference in their finally winning a championship. You always hear that God was watching over them, had a plan for them, or other variations of these statements. Apparently, God has nothing better to do than to intervene in a basketball game, so that a particular player can win a championship.[3] Perhaps his team won with a last-second shot at the buzzer. The shot would not have gone in, but God made it go in. Why He did not do this favor for an equally deserving player on the opposing team, or save a devoutly religious person (who prayed in church regularly but perished in The World Trade Center), is not answered. But who are we mortals to question the will of God?

Sometimes, people believe things out of convenience, or because it is the only way to make sense of their lives and to move forward. Often, an accident will leave a person without limbs or sight; sometimes a person is *born* with a terrible handicap. He will say that everything happens for a reason, and that God chose him to be that way, so that he could help and inspire others. I greatly admire and respect Nick Vujicic, the man born without arms and legs. He is self-sufficient, a real go-getter, and a truly friendly, upbeat, and happy person who gives sermons and motivational speeches throughout the world. He believes that being born this way was God's purpose for him. He is a preacher and a true believer. First of all, if there *were* a God, I would not consider Him to be a good one for allowing anyone to live like this. I would consider it to be a curse of the highest magnitude. Secondly, Vujicic got the way he is through an accident or "mistake" of birth, *not* because any supreme being had any divine plan for him. But if Vujicic believes what he does, so as to make sense out of his misfortune, then his belief is a positive thing.

There are countless religions in the world, and the fact that so many religions exist indicates that all have different interpretations. But religion is not music, where two pianists offering different interpretations of a Beethoven sonata can be equally convincing. God either exists, or He does not; and an event either took place, or it did not. We may not know the right answer, but this does not alter the fact that there *is* an answer. I realize that some people wiggle out of the issue of a supreme being by talking about a life force or universal force. They can appease the atheists and agnostics by claiming that they don't necessarily believe in an old man with a beard,[4] but when speaking with believers, they can claim that this nebulous "universal force" is God.

Most religions disagree on major issues. Christians believe that Jesus Christ was the son of God, and that He was sacrificed on the cross to save the rest of us from our sins. The Jews do not believe Jesus was the son of God, and a religious Jew once told me that God would never have had His own son sacrificed. Obviously, both beliefs contradict each other. This is why I think it would be a waste to believe something on *faith*, and spend my whole life practicing a religion based on these beliefs.

Admittedly, I know nothing about religion, the Bible, or anything related to religion. But I do recognize all the contradictions and hypocrisy surrounding it. Whatever the true answer may be regarding God's existence, whether or not He intervenes in events on Earth, whether there is a Heaven or Hell, what the purpose of our lives is, or whether there is an afterlife, I do know that the very essence of religion has to do with being and/or striving to be a good person, and that loving each other is its highest ideal. Any religion that preaches the sacrifice of people and animals, or the killing of people of another religion and/or those that do not share their beliefs is a contradiction in terms. Similarly, for the captured al-Qaeda or Taliban members requesting to pray and to practice their religion, or for Saddam Hussein — before he was hanged — to evoke the name of Allah and call the people who opposed him "the enemies of God" is ludicrous. How religious can mass murderers, rapists, and torturers be?

From what I have written, it might seem incongruous that I greatly admired Mother Teresa. Even though we had different beliefs, she not only "talked the talk," but "walked the walk." And she acted in ways consistent with her beliefs. When she visited Gracie Mansion, she refused lemonade, because the people she was helping in the slums of Calcutta had no access to it. She did the things she did in life because she believed that they were the right things to do. What a contrast that is to so many of the bad people of the world, who pray in houses of worship on a regular basis, consider themselves religious and men of God, but continue to perform atrocities in their everyday lives.

CHAPTER 2

A Higher Form Of Life

One day, I had a gig playing the piano for a church service. A large insect appeared on the floor. A "religious" woman, who was a member of the staff, shrieked, "A creepy-crawly!" and proceeded to commit a socially acceptable form of murder by stomping out its life. The insect had posed no threat to anyone. Had someone thought the sight of it to be too "ugly," had someone thought it could cause disease, or had someone simply felt it had no right to occupy the floor of a house of God (who "created" it), it could easily have been evacuated by placing a paper underneath it, and carrying it outside to its more hospitable habitat. The door leading outside happened to have been right near where the insect had been.

I have witnessed children stomping out the life of ants. Ants are tiny, but nevertheless industrious and productive critters. I have seen them carrying breadcrumbs which were much bigger — and heavier — than they were, back to their colonies. If they are in their natural habitat, they pose little threat to humans. Yet killing them, even merely for kicks, is considered morally insignificant. After all, they're *only* ants.

During the presidential debates, John Kerry went duck hunting, and even bragged about shooting down a duck. Not one person reacted with disapproval, much less revulsion at the murder of an innocent animal. After all, duck hunting is a "sport." If someone cooked the bird and ate it, he could argue that he was killing the bird as an act of survival, in the same manner that animals kill other animals to survive. But this was merely a game of target practice.

Michael Vick got into a lot of trouble for running a dogfighting operation. He did time in jail, and this threatened his football career. People have wondered how any decent person could take part in, much less derive pleasure from, such a barbaric activity... even though bullfighting — with the purpose of killing the bull — is a national "sport" in Spain, and cockfighting is accepted as part of the "culture" in some Latin American countries. But when one kills a human, even an evil one who has tried to harm — or has harmed — an innocent person or people, he can receive the death penalty or life in prison. No doubt this is because humans are a "higher form of life." It also has to do with *size.* If a person kills an ant — even if he announces his act to the world — it is considered so inconsequential as to be comical. Killing a dog or an elephant can get you a fine, and possibly a jail sentence (depending on how many dogs or elephants you kill), but killing a person can result in a long jail sentence, life imprisonment, or the death penalty...even if by killing this person, one could be saving countless others from being killed by him. Interesting....Let's examine the meaning of "a higher form of life."

What *is* a higher form of life? I don't know, but based on our laws, and what is widely considered to be "right" or "proper," it must have something to do with size and with brain complexity. It must also have something to do with "reasoning ability," and the ability "to know right from wrong." As mentioned in the previous chapter, there are those that argue that a hurricane, tsunami, tornado, or an earthquake is not "evil." It just *is.* This is just nature being nature, regardless of whether or not a Haitian baby (who had no choice as to where he was born) is killed by a building falling on his head, or by disease resulting from the sewage and lack of sanitation in the aftermath of the earthquake. This can't be blamed on *God,* because — as already mentioned — He will not interfere in the occurrence of events, especially those relating to *nature*...unless, of course, some-one is saved. Then God will garner all the credit.

A shark that kills a person, it can be argued, is not *evil* for eating a person who happens to present himself close to dinner time. It is just acting consistent with its nature. It didn't kill the person because that person happened to have been a bastard, a murderer, or didn't pay his income taxes. The person could have been a saint, but the shark does not discriminate. It's just that *law of survival* thing. But had it been *me* whom the shark was trying to eat, I would owe it to myself to do everything within my power to see that I survived, even if it meant killing the shark. And if that happened, I would not have incurred any associated guilt whatsoever.

Getting back to what constitutes "a higher form of life," I've already mentioned that it must have something to do with *size*, and it must have something to do with brain complexity. A seeing-eye dog is invaluable and priceless to its blind owner. Similarly, a monkey can be an invaluable asset to a paraplegic. The tasks they perform require a definite level of intelligence. The level of their intelligence is certainly more developed than that of a newborn infant, who is *totally* dependent (even though their future intellectual capacity could have been far greater than that of the guide dog or monkey). But this cannot be said of a severely retarded person, even though he would be regarded as "a higher form of life." So intelligence, per se, is not the total barometer. The fact that we are "human" is the real criterion for considering us "a higher form of life" than animals.

CHAPTER 3

The Anatomy Of Evil

I n *Random House Webster's College Dictionary,* there is a plethora of definitions for the word *evil.* Some of them are: 1) morally wrong or bad; immoral; wicked; 2) marked by anger, irritability, irascibility; 3) harm, mischief, misfortune; anything causing injury or harm.

The first one is correct, but it does not define "morally wrong or bad, immoral, or wicked." The second definition listed can be considered a characteristic shared by evil people, but falls short as a defining element. I have seen people who were angry, irritable, and irascible, but were not evil. And sometimes normally pleasant and "good" people can exhibit characteristics of the above, even though it is not the norm. Part of the third definition, "harm, mischief, and misfortune" suggests that a situation or circumstance can be considered evil. "Anything causing injury or harm" can refer to an earthquake, hurricane, tornado, or tsunami, and could definitely be characterized as being evil...even though these are *natural* occurrences, which do not possess cognition and intent.

Some people believe a "supreme being" or God is behind these events, but I don't. If one substitutes any*one* for any*thing,* the person causing injury or harm can sometimes be considered evil, but sometimes not. The definition is not addressing the *intent* of the perpetrator. A drunk driver who kills innocent people can rightfully be considered a murderer, but he or she is often not an evil person (even though the outcome of his or her stupidity and carelessness turned out the same as with a driver who *purposely* intended to cause harm).

Try this one on for size: An evil person is not only one who perpetrates death and/or suffering on innocent people or animals; he or she *intends* to and derives pleasure from doing so. Evil people have no hearts or consciences. People who have done bad things, acknowledged their mistakes, vowed not to repeat the things that they considered to be wrong, and feel sorry for what they did are not evil.

I have made more than my share of mistakes throughout my life, and have done things that were wrong. That's part of what it means to be human. Some of the things I have done haunt me to this day, and I wish I could erase them from history. But there are some things I would be incapable of doing.

Let us say that I had the opportunity to rob an elderly blind woman on the street, to swindle an old senile woman out of her life savings, to sexually molest a child, or to torture an animal. For the sake of this example, we will say that there is no possibility that I would be caught. But I would still be incapable of doing any of the above, for the simple reason that I would not be able to live with my conscience. An evil person would do all of the above, and feel no regret or remorse. In addition, he would derive pleasure, not only from his ill-gotten gains (in the case of stealing money or valuables), but from destroying property, causing death, and/or inflicting severe pain. If an opportunity arose to beat and rob a helpless person on the spur of the moment, they would not hesitate to do so, as long as they didn't get caught. In addition, they would also act premeditatedly in other situations. It would come as naturally to them as drinking a glass of water. People have been known to murder their families, then go out and party as the bodies decomposed in their homes.

People who don't personally commit or order egregious acts against the innocent, but celebrate such occurrences when they happen (such as the Muslims across the river in New Jersey who were cheering as they watched the Twin Towers falling on 9/11) are evil, as well. Many evil people do not publicly celebrate when a tragedy occurs, and keep their opinions to themselves, however happy they might be. If they are not *physically* committing or ordering egregious acts, they certainly cannot be prosecuted and imprisoned for their thoughts.

One time, I stopped at a service station on the highway to fill up my tank. The woman I had to pay for the gas was wearing a jacket with a swastika on it. I thought that I must be mistaken, because this could not be possible. How could someone publicly celebrate pure evil, the unspeakable horrors of the Holocaust, and the intended annihilation of all the Jewish people in the world (as well as the future generations who were never born, as a result)? But it wasn't until I had driven off that I realized she really *was* wearing a swastika. I felt revulsion, and I ended up hating myself for giving her my business, and for not saying or doing something.

I started fantasizing about a Jewish man stopping at this same gas station an hour later. His entire family was exterminated in the ovens of Auschwitz. He sees what this woman is proudly displaying, and his brain suddenly starts to feel like it is exploding, as all the visual memories rush into it. He snaps. He takes out his sawed-off shotgun and blows her into oblivion.

Would *I* have killed this woman? No…not as long as she wasn't trying to personally harm me, and wasn't in the act of harming or trying to harm someone else. But I *would* be happy if I learned there was one less of her kind in the world. And if I had witnessed the gentleman blowing her away, knew *why* he had done it, and was subsequently asked by the police if I had witnessed the incident and could identify the perpetrator, I would in no way help them. We're talking about a woman who proudly wears an emblem celebrating the torture, murder, and annihilation of Jews. Had this woman been one of the guards at any of the concentration camps, she would have participated with alacrity in all of the atrocities, and would no doubt kill Jews here, if she were able to do so with impunity.

For those who would say I was advocating the murder of a *human being*, I would first refer you to the section of this book where I speak about "higher forms of life." I would also point out that many people, such as former President Jimmy Carter, are hunters, and also eat animals and wear leather shoes. But if that doesn't make my point, I would suggest that the woman in the gas station was not human at all, but *sub*human, i.e. an animal. And if it's not morally wrong to hunt bears, deer, and ducks, why is it wrong to hunt Nazis?[5]

Do convicted sex offenders and pedophiles have a right to live wherever they want? I have heard of some laws stating that they must keep a specified distance from places such as schools, or wherever children congregate. I don't know whether or not there are any laws specifying how close an offender may *live* to children. I *do* know that there have been instances where offenders lived next door to — or in close proximity to — families with young children.

There are those who will argue that a sex offender has to live *somewhere*. "If he has been released from prison," some would argue, "he has already done his time and paid his debt to society, and should now be allowed to live wherever he chooses."

But being released from prison does not mean he is "rehabilitated." There *have* been examples of criminals who have been rehabilitated, turned their lives around, and become good, upstanding citizens. But being a sexual predator is an *illness*. Doing time because of the despicable things they have done does not "cure" them. It merely keeps them away from vulnerable children during the time of their incarceration. Being released on parole has proved a sham on many occasions — and even if this individual were placed on parole for a specified number of years after his release, what about all the time he is *un*supervised?

People might argue that this individual might have been ordered to undergo therapy or psychiatric treatment as one of the conditions of his parole. But again…what about all the time he is *un*supervised? And as for psychiatric treatment…psychiatry is a *very* inexact science. If one has a tumor, it can be removed, and the person is cured; people likewise get their tonsils taken out. We can objectively verify that the treatment was successful. This is not the case with psychiatry, where one is dealing with a cornucopia of nebulous suppositions and assessments. The human mind, emotions, and motivations are not easily deciphered. If everything were so cut and dried, why are the multitudes of people who have had, or are still undergoing, psychiatric treatment, still so dysfunctional?

What do you do if a convicted sex offender moves into the house next door, and you have young children? The law states he has a right to live there, but what about the parents' right not to have the safety of their children put in jeopardy? What obligation does the criminal justice system — that our taxes are paying for — have? What culpability do they have if the sex offender that they released molests children again?

You and your neighbors should inform the predator that he has to move. If that does not work, you should get signed petitions, and contact your congressman, and any other politicians whom you feel could help. A lawsuit could be filed, contesting this individual's right to live next door to your children.

If all legal measures have been exhausted, I would welcome the burning down of his house, as long as no one is inside, and the fire could not spread to other homes. I personally would not do this if I weren't 100% certain I wouldn't be caught. But I would certainly welcome this occurrence, and be thankful to whoever did it.[6] To those who would argue that burning down someone's house is illegal, I would ask them, "Would you rather do something illegal to safeguard a loved one, or follow the rule of law, and put your daughter in jeopardy of getting kidnapped, raped, sodomized, or murdered?"

Some would dismiss me as a militant kook with a screw loose. What if this person, for argument's sake, is truly rehabilitated? To answer that question, I would ask, "What if you're waiting on line to board a plane, and a man named Muhammad Zaid Abdul-Azziz is next to you. He is acting in a way that you deem to be suspicious. You are very frightened, but also afraid that if you relay your suspicions to the authorities, and engage in "racial profiling," Muslims will consider you a racist. What if it turns out that this man had no intent to do anything wrong? Would you rather be embarrassed and safe, or not "offend" someone, but be dead?

There are different categories of evil. Bernard Madoff would not have beaten and robbed an elderly and helpless person on the street. Yet his deliberate and premeditated actions destroyed the lives of many people. The fact that some of his victims were charitable religious institutions of his own Jewish faith makes his actions all the more despicable. A heartless mugger or rapist might have claimed fewer victims, but I would place him on the same hierarchical level as Madoff. Both are examples of people who exhibited a depraved indifference to the pain and suffering of others, regardless of whose actions resulted in the most widespread destruction.

On what rung of the *evil* ladder do *emotional sadists* stand? I am referring to teachers, parents, or adults who will tell a child (who is not misbehaving or acting up) that they will never amount to anything, and who will implicitly say that in a world of producers and achievers, they are *not enough.*[7] How about people at work who will sabotage your work out of jealousy, to climb the corporate ladder ahead of you? I heard of a woman who had her entire college dissertation, along with months of work, wiped out deliberately from her computer. Sometimes cruel, malicious, disgusting, and despicable people cannot be classified as *evil*. They don't kill people, cut off limbs with machetes (as in Sierra Leone), rape and murder entire villages for purposes of "racial cleansing," etc. There are many cruel people out there who are not necessarily evil, but sometimes they come close. Sometimes, it's a fine line. I would place the person who erased the computer files in the *evil* category.

What about the cliché that there is some good in everyone? Well, it sounds good, but I would disagree. Some people are just *bad*. I anticipate being criticized for stating this, because most people would say that nothing is "black and white" and that there are areas of gray. Just because a person has some redeeming or human qualities, does not mean that they cannot be considered a *fundamentally* bad person. The determining factor is the long-standing pattern of their behavior and the totality of what makes them who they are.

I watched the interview of John Gotti, Jr. by Steve Croft on *60 Minutes* (February, 2011) with fascination. Gotti, Jr. is a *bad guy*. This is one guy you do *not* want to fuck with. But during the interview, he was engaging and pleasant. His love for and loyalty to his family were obvious.

CHAPTER 4

Taking The Law Into Our Own Hands

ARE REVENGE AND VIGILANTISM JUSTIFIED?

The law, however flawed, has been designed and written to mitigate disputes and to mete out "justice." It can be thought of as a kind of workable encyclopedia of morality...even though its practitioners do not exactly hold a stellar reputation in the morality and ethics department. In the mockery of justice, aka the O.J. Simpson trial, a team of skillful but corrupt lawyers succeeded in securing a *not guilty* verdict for a murderer guilty beyond all reasonable doubt. Marcia Clark, one of the prosecuting attorneys, urged people not to lose faith in the US justice system (even though it failed miserably on this occasion).

When justice fails, what do we say to the people who are directly affected?

∞

A beautiful, intelligent, loving, and vibrant little girl is abducted by an evil monster. She is raped, sodomized, and decapitated. Other body parts are cut off, as well. The parents' lives are forever destroyed, and they are living through a personal Hell of such magnitude that they can see no hope of ever coming out of the abyss. They are broken and shattered, and can hardly perform their necessary daily tasks. Doing the laundry, ironing, vacuuming, preparing a meal, going to the grocery store, getting out of bed in the morning, taking a shower, brushing their teeth, and getting dressed all require too much physical and emotional energy. But they continue to live, even though they have died a thousand deaths.

The murderer is caught, and DNA proves that the semen found on the little girl's body was his. The attorney representing the parents makes a mistake, the judge declares a mistrial, and the murderer is exonerated on a technicality. The judge explains that the "integrity" of the American judicial justice system supersedes the occasional incidents when guilty people are set free. "That's the price we pay for living in a democracy," he says. "Our judicial system is not perfect, but it is better than that of any other country."

As he leaves the courtroom, the murderer passes where the parents are sitting. He shoots a sly smile at them, and chuckles. This is too much for them to bear. They wanted this individual, at the very least, to be locked up and put away, so that another parent would not have to experience what they are going through. But this animal mocks their pain, and takes pleasure in it. Do the parents have a right to take matters into their own hands and go after the killer? "No," scream the bleeding heart liberals. "By killing the murderer, it would make *us* murderers. After all, two wrongs don't make a right. Only God can create a life, so only God should take a life. And besides, this individual will be punished for his sins in the 'afterlife.'" This self-righteous gobbledygook sounds impressive, but what do you say to the parents? What *is* the answer?

The answer is "no." The parents should not go after the murderer if there is any possibility that they could be caught. If they *are*, they will go to jail for a long time, thus adding insult to their injury. In addition, a perverse and grotesque mockery of "justice" would have been turned upside down and inside out. However...if by killing or having the murderer killed, the parents can escape detection and prosecution, it would be completely moral to kill the murderer...and by doing so, they might save the lives of future victims, and spare the *destruction* of the lives of their loved ones.

The liberals will say that we cannot take the law into our own hands, but as this is being written, we all received the good news that

Osama bin Laden was finally killed. I didn't hear any complaints from civilized society.

THE BERNHARD GOETZ CASE

Recently, I read the obituary of James Ramseur in *The New York Times*. Remember him? He was one of the punks who mugged Bernhard Goetz on the #2 train in Manhattan on December 22, 1984. Bernhard Goetz was the engineer who had been mugged in the past, and decided that he was going to do something about it if he were placed in that situation again. Sure enough, he was. This time, he had a gun, and his muggers weren't so lucky. Another one of the punks, Darrell Cabey, was paralyzed. The incident polarized the city, in a way that the O.J. Simpson trial was later to do. Part of the situation became a *black* against *white* issue, rather than an issue of a hard-working and peaceful person who had had enough, and wasn't going to take it anymore. The late William Kunstler, and his protégé, Ron Kuby, represented the muggers. People had said Goetz was crazy, and had used excessive force. They pointed to the comment he is said to have uttered when he had already shot one of the muggers: "You don't look so bad. Here's another."

It is public record that Ramseur continued his life of crime, even after he was thwarted on this occasion. He was convicted of raping and sodomizing a woman. While reading his obituary, I remember daydreaming about someone studying his life, and writing his biography... in the same way that people have done with da Vinci, Michelangelo, Beethoven, Lincoln, Einstein, Ayn Rand and other supreme achievers of history. The absurdity of someone wasting their life studying the life of a totally worthless person was quite depressing. But to a lesser extent, this is what apologists and lawyers of evil people do when they try to explain away these creatures' transgressions with tales of their improper toilet training, their parents' dysfunctional marriage, their broken home, ad infinitum.

At the time of the Goetz incident, I was working during the summer, and was teamed up with a co-worker who happened to be black. I asked him what he felt about what Goetz had done. He said he thought Goetz was crazy. I asked him what he thought would have happened to Goetz had he not had a gun. He said, "They probably would have beaten him up."

I then asked him, "What would you do if you saw your mother being beaten up, and you had a gun?"

"I would probably shoot them," he said.

I have never met Bernhard Goetz, but would love to shake his hand and say, "Thank you." He not only saved his own ass, but did something for every decent and law-abiding citizen in the city. I'm sorry he had to suffer through all the ramifications in the aftermath.

VIOLENCE IN THE ABSENCE OF A PHYSICAL THREAT

Professional athletes are idolized and looked up to by millions of people. They have achieved a level of fame and financial status alien to the overwhelming majority of people. People become rabid fans of various teams and athletes. They buy their jerseys, scream in ecstasy, and celebrate when their team wins. Some fans live and die by the victories and defeats of their team. What this says about their self-esteem — or how a team from their home town that wins a championship somehow makes *them* better — is another issue.

But the fame and admiration of certain athletes is also a double-edged sword. Even phenomenally gifted and successful athletes have had "You suck" said to them when they lose, commit an error, or strike out. If it could be said to Don Mattingly, it could be said to anyone. Athletes have been instructed to turn a deaf ear toward what any fan should say to them, and never to go into the stands. Most athletes have the discipline to adhere to this if it is just a case of being booed, or even heckled. If some lowlife who happens to be, perhaps, a truck driver or factory worker (and drunk at the same time) is saying that they stink, a mature player considers the source, and doesn't let it affect him too much. The jerk is paying to see *him*, not the other way around. He wishes that *he* could be a famous athlete who never has to worry about paying his bills, who sees his name in the paper regularly, and is admired by millions. He also knows that he would *never* be able to do or to achieve what this athlete has. He derives his self-esteem — or more aptly, *pseudo* self-esteem — from the exploits of his chosen team.

But what of the situations where the taunts become more personal? There have been situations where a player's mother or loved one has just died, and believe it or not, fans have teased and taunted a player at these times. Former pitcher David Wells comes to mind. Granted, only human shit would be capable of this, but it does happen. And for an otherwise level-headed player to suddenly snap when confronted with such vile scum is understandable, if expensive.

My advice to the athletes would be to have security remove the identified person. Especially if the player is a star, and if he threatens not to continue playing unless that individual is removed, there is a good chance his wishes will be granted. John McEnroe had an annoying fan removed from the stadium. The player should explain to law enforcement in a calm and respectful but direct manner that the individual is saying highly offensive things about him and/or his family...and that he doesn't want to have to do something that he is going to regret. As much as it would be justifiable for the lowlife to get his ass seriously kicked, the athlete would suffer far more serious consequences. Sometimes, a person *wants* the athlete to physically assault him, so that he can then sue a multi-millionaire.

SHOULD WE TORTURE TERRORISTS?

As this is being written, The United States is currently holding terrorists at its detention camp at Guantánamo Bay. Is it morally right to torture the prisoners if information gained from them could lead to the capture of other terrorists or could abort a future attack? President Obama has stated that The United States does not torture prisoners, but during this debate, the following scenario has been raised: Suppose a catastrophic attack were imminent. A terrorist is believed to know a code that could defuse a nuclear bomb capable of wiping out an entire country. Is it okay to torture him? A person on a news program answered, "No." But what is the right answer?

First of all, in cases of whether or not to torture a prisoner, one must have some important questions answered (which were not even raised in the debates): Would the torturing of a given terrorist — however morally valid it may be — result in almost certain retaliation, killing many innocent people? How do we know whether or not the terrorist would be giving truthful information? Terrorists certainly have no moral issues regarding lying to the enemy. Assuming the terrorist is telling the truth, is the information verifiable? With regard to the terrorist who knows the code that can defuse the nuclear bomb, no one asked the question "If we tortured this terrorist, would it be certain that he would give us the code?"

As we have seen, some terrorists would rather die and be a "martyr" than do anything that could help the enemy. But if we know that by torturing this terrorist, we would get the correct code to defuse the bomb, not only is it morally proper to torture this individual — it would be immoral *not* to. Whose life is more important, a mass murderer's, or the lives of thousands of innocent people? Similarly, if by torturing an individual (who would kill us unhesitatingly if given the chance), we could receive *verifiably* truthful information that could thwart future attacks and/or lead us to other terrorists, it would be our moral obligation to get this information any way we could.

Mother Teresa would have disagreed, as would other "people of God." They would view the torture or killing of a terrorist as immoral, even if by doing so, we would have *saved* many lives. They would not consider *intention* a crime unless the crime were carried out. But the *prevention* would be. Unfortunately, the latter would be too late, had we not intervened. As Ayn Rand has said, "We have no moral obligation to participate in our own destruction."

WATERING THE LEAVES

Recently, a situation involving American troops and the Taliban in Afghanistan was in the news. US troops took cell phone photos of their buddies urinating on dead Taliban fighters, and the videos apparently turned up on YouTube. This situation provided a lot of fodder for daytime radio talk show debate. As I write, it seems these young men are facing serious trouble, and even prison sentences for their act (the "desecration" of human corpses). How "desecrating" a (former) living thing that was so vile and evil constitutes desecration, I don't understand. As one person who called in to a radio talk show rightfully pointed out, these were the people who had decapitated Daniel Pearl.

This all takes me back to my discussion of what constitutes a "higher form of life." If the troops had urinated on ants, rats, or worms, had bragged about it, *and* videotaped it, the only thing they might have gotten in trouble for was displaying their penises and performing a "lewd" act, *not* for urinating on the ants, rats, or worms. Why not? Because they're *only* ants, rats, or worms. How can you compare this to urinating on a *person*? I would like to challenge anyone to rationally explain to me why a Taliban fighter constitutes "a higher form of life" than an ant, rat, or worm. I will go even further, by suggesting that urinating — or defecating — on a Taliban corpse is a non-issue. It can even be thought of as a *positive* thing. The Taliban, and similar "people" are so depraved, and have caused so much pain to the loved ones of the innocent lives they have destroyed, that urinating or defecating on their remains can act as a catharsis...even though the urine and shit are of far greater value than the bodies (dead *or* alive) they'd be covering.

CHAPTER 5

Poetic Justice

Poetic justice doesn't happen very often, but when it does, it feels so good! Several years ago, someone was being mugged on the subway, and a Good Samaritan came to the rescue. I believe the mugger was shot to death. The Good Samaritan got away, and law enforcement urged him to turn himself in. When asked if he had anything to say to the Good Samaritan, the intended victim offered his perfect advice: "If you don't turn yourself in, they won't find you." And as far as I know, the Good Samaritan was never "caught." Why a Good Samaritan would be urged to turn himself in to face punishment for saving an innocent person is beyond me. I guess you'd have to be a bleeding heart liberal to know the answer... unless it was they or a loved one who was mugged.

I urge anyone who should happen to be attacked, and saved by a Good Samaritan, *never* to identify this person, or to give a diametrically opposed description...as was done in a similar situation in the movie *Death Wish*.

∞

One of the unwritten laws of baseball is that pitchers must protect their hitters. Let's say a batter gets a multitude of hits off a pitcher — including, perhaps, a home run...or even a grand slam. It is customary to receive a "brushback" pitch, or even to get hit...the rationale being that no batter can get the better of him (the pitcher) without suffering the consequences. If the element of *fear* is put into the equation, perhaps that will make it more difficult for the batter to get a hit. When he is worried about being thrown at, his concentration is no longer undivided. Another situation in which pitchers throw at hitters is when they believe they have been "shown up" — as when a hitter stands at home plate admiring a home run he has just hit. But when a hitter is thrown at, it is protocol for the opposing pitcher to throw at the first hitter he faces. Often, he is even instructed to do so by his manager, with the understanding that his teammates will "have his back" and protect him should a brawl ensue. He faces the possibility of getting thrown out of the game (especially if he has received a prior warning), but not retaliating is viewed as the catalyst for future problems. It is construed as *weakness.*

There are too many nuances to state that brushback pitches, or even hitting a batter, should *never* be justified. But throwing a ball at over ninety mph at someone's head could have catastrophic consequences. I believe that most people would agree that *deliberately* throwing at a batter's head, especially with the intent to cause harm, is unacceptable. But suppose this happened, and the batter's helmet was the only thing that saved him from getting a concussion or losing his life. One time, this happened in real life. The batter then bunted down the first base line, and ran over the pitcher who was covering the bag.

But an even more delicious scenario would be if the batter hit a pitch that struck the pitcher in the head. It is so difficult to precisely control where a ball is hit. Pitchers are often adept at inducing a batter to pop up. Sometimes a ball is hit really hard, but fouled off, or hit directly to the center fielder for an out. So even if a batter deliberately tried to hit a pitcher, it could never be proved. And because of all the variables mentioned, he could never be held liable even if he *did* try to hit the pitcher. Sometimes it has worked out for the *pitcher,* when a ball came directly at him, and he ended up catching it for an out. What I am saying is that a pitcher who deliberately throws at a batter's head — who then gets hit in the head *himself* by the ball hit by that batter — is a situation that constitutes the epitome of poetic justice. Another example is when someone tries to mug someone, and gets mugged himself.

Here is another scenario: A driver, whom we'll call Driver A, is driving up a winding mountain road. There are no barricades, even though the road is on the edge of a cliff with a steep drop-off. Aware of the treacherous nature of the route, he drives carefully and obeys the posted speed limit. A driver from the rear, whom we'll call Driver B, approaches and starts honking his horn. He has a different idea as to how fast the car in front of him (Driver A) should be going. Normally, he would just have passed him, but because of the constant sharp turns, approaching vehicles can't be seen. So he just honks to try to intimidate Driver A into driving faster.

Driver A *is* intimidated, and starts driving five mph above the speed limit. But the honking persists. Driver B attempts to pass, but suddenly slams on the brakes and gets back into his lane, when an approaching vehicle appears. This enrages him, and the honking escalates to bumping Driver A from the rear. Driver A is terrified. He doesn't know whether to risk his life by driving faster, or to risk his life by *not* driving faster. Finally, he stops the car to induce Driver B to pass him on the left. But Driver B interprets this as Driver A playing games with him and holding him back in order to retaliate. He floors the engine to try to pass, but again, does not see an approaching vehicle, as the road turns 90 degrees in front of him.

He makes it back into his lane by a hair, but by now he is going ballistic. He is screaming obscenities, sitting on the horn, and slamming the vehicle ahead of him with great force. Driver A is panicking, and in fear for his life. Again, Driver B tries to pass, and pulls along to the left side of Driver A. As he does so, he rams the side of his car into Driver A in an attempt to push him into the rocks that jut out at the side of the right lane. But he doesn't notice the Mack truck approaching around the bend. Driver A sees the approaching truck a micro-second before Driver B does, because Driver B is looking and screaming at him. In the next instant, Driver B sees the oncoming truck. He cannot turn back into the right lane, as Driver A is still alongside him (even though he has just floored the accelerator). He turns sharply to the left to avoid the head-on collision, but in doing so, drives right off the cliff. For a few seconds, there is silence, then a deafening explosion accompanied by a fiery inferno. Flames are shooting up into the sky, and it is all so much more impressive than any fireworks display on the 4th of July.

Out of harm's way, Driver A stops to observe the display. An ear to ear smile reflexively brightens his normally staid features. He high-fives his girlfriend sitting next to him in the passenger's seat. No words are spoken, but his look says, "Whew, that was a close one, wasn't it?" For the first time in his life, the money he will have to shell out for the body work on his car doesn't bother him. He views it as a souvenir of his good fortune, and a totally acceptable trade-off. The end result was an ample reward for the fifteen minutes of terror he has just endured.

In the next day's paper, he reads about the carnage. The corpse was charred beyond recognition, but dental records revealed the identity of the driver...a career criminal who was in and out of jail for armed robbery, as well as for assault and battery. Most recently, he had been serving a term for child molestation, but was let out early on parole despite the tearful pleas of the mother of one of his victims.

In the days ahead, Driver A constantly receives comments on how happy he looks. Usually a serious guy, his current ubiquitous smile is rather conspicuous by comparison. "What's got into you?" asks one of the guys in the locker room at the gym. "He must be getting laid," another guy chimes in. He's right, but he doesn't know that Driver A has been having sex all along. But now, it has taken on a much more celebratory air. Poetic justice is a great thing to celebrate, especially since it doesn't happen very often.

CHAPTER 6

Dealing With
Criminals

I once read a Cindy Adams (I believe) column in *The New York Post*. She was in Saudi Arabia, and someone had left a wallet full of money on a counter at an airport terminal. After witnessing it, she encountered the very same wallet — completely undisturbed — in the same place, a long time later. I don't remember if it was a day or two or a week later, but the exact amount of time it was lying there is not the issue. The issue is that it was still there. I remember being fascinated by the situation, because this could never happen here. If you placed a wallet full of money on a counter in Grand Central Station, it would be gone the moment you turned your head…guaranteed. And often, the criminals don't even *wait* for you to turn your head or have a lapse of concentration. They'll grab it *from* you.

The reason the wallet was still there at the airport in Saudi Arabia is because the penalty for theft is to have your hand cut off. It's not a foolproof deterrent, of course, but would certainly make the average person think twice as to whether the risks outweigh the punishment if they were caught.

I have mixed thoughts regarding this law. On the one hand, I am fed up with crime, having personally experienced more than my share. I have no problem with someone in need *asking* me for money or food if they are legitimately in need. In some instances, I might give it to them. But taking something that does not belong to you — especially by force — is another issue. I totally believe that if the consequences are great, then it *is* a deterrent. I don't know of anyone who would choose money over a limb.

My concern regarding this extreme — and some might say, barbaric — punishment, is the question: "Is it 100% verifiable that the wallet (money) was taken for personal gain?" Suppose the person who took the wallet knew who dropped it, and intended to look for and find the owner, so as to return it? Suppose the taker of the wallet did not want the money for himself, but had starving children, and the money in the wallet was the only way he could buy food for them? Or suppose he thought he had dropped his own wallet, and that the one he took was his…because it was the same color and size?[8]

For these reasons, I would not be in favor of cutting off someone's hand; if a mistake were made, a hand could not be grown back, and no amount of money could atone for a missing body part. In addition, the respective value (monetary and sentimental) of various stolen items would not have been taken into account.

How *should* we deal with criminals who commit crimes against us? Rather than *just* sending the criminals to jail, they should have to compensate the victim(s) so severely as to make it a deterrent for any and all robberies and/or assaults. And perhaps the criminals should be allowed a choice between staggering financial remuneration to their victims, an extremely long jail sentence, or — depending on the magnitude of the crime — a sentence without the possibility of parole.

On one of the news programs, the topic was a "three strikes, you're out" policy. A person received a long, or possibly a life sentence after he stole a slice of pizza from a child.[9] But this was the person's *third* offense. The whole tone of the program focused on the question, "How can you put someone away for stealing a slice of pizza?" Hearing this question out of context would naturally summon outrage. But this person was jailed for the *cumulative* crimes he had committed, and he was aware of the law beforehand. He should not have stolen anything the first time, and even after the second time, he was given a free pass. Needless to say, I didn't lose any sleep over his plight.

Another situation involved a man who kept having his house

broken into. Reporting this to law enforcement didn't work. Finally, he rigged up a device that shot the thief in the leg and crippled him. I don't remember the details, but the homeowner was severely punished. On the news, the thief said that he didn't condone what he had done, but that was no reason to cripple a man for life.

One isolated incident is too many, but if it doesn't happen again, one can rationalize and say that these kind of ugly things are a part of life, and that maybe this filled his "quota." But if the homeowner were continuously getting robbed, and tried to do the right thing by going to law enforcement, but to no avail, I would like to ask the thief what the homeowner was *supposed* to have done …resign himself to being wiped out financially, as well as having his life and that of his family jeopardized? [10]

As you might have surmised, I do *not* like criminals, and I do not want to hear about their upbringing being the cause (excuse) for their crimes. I value the safety, sovereignty, and rights of decent law-abiding people.

CHAPTER 7

The Death Penalty

The debate as to whether or not the death penalty is just, is like the debate over abortion and the Palestinian/Israeli conflict. It will *never* be resolved. Too many people feel so strongly pro and con about their own position that the two sides will never meet…especially when you throw in religion, and have *that* on your side.

In the August 16, 2012 edition of *The New York Times*, William Yardley wrote an obituary for Hugo Bedau, the philosopher who had opposed the death penalty for being immoral, unjust, and ineffective. Yardley writes that in a pamphlet entitled "The Case Against the Death Penalty" (distributed by the American Civil Liberties Union), Bedau said that it failed to deter crime, was fraught with racial bias, wrongful convictions, and excessive financial costs, and that it was ultimately an act of "barbarity." He writes, in a section marked "Unfairness": "The history of capital punishment in American society clearly shows the desire to mitigate the harshness of this penalty by narrowing its scope. Discretion, whether authored by statutes or by their silence, has been the main vehicle to this end. But when discretion is used, as it always has been, to mark for death the poor, the friendless, the uneducated, the members of racial minorities and the despised, then discretion becomes injustice. Thoughtful citizens, who in contemplating capital punishment in the abstract might support it, must condemn it in actual practice."

I respect Bedaus' views, and many of his points are valid. I also respect people who oppose the death penalty because it conflicts with their religious beliefs. I'm sure that these people do not want crimes to be committed, any more than I do. Yes, there *are* problems with the death penalty. Before DNA testing, innocent people were put to death, as were poor people who could not afford to pay for adequate legal representation. People have been put to death — not just rotted in jail — for crimes they did not commit, because they were framed, because of mistaken identity, and because of corruption. And unlike a life prison sentence, once a mistake is made, and an innocent person is put to death, you can't bring him back.

But Bedaus' last statement that I quoted leaves me with some questions. Is Bedau condemning capital punishment only in actual practice? Regarding his reference to those who contemplate it in the abstract, is he suggesting that *if* capital punishment were free of all the injustices and inequities he cites, that it *could* be a viable punishment? The question isn't answered in the quotes in the obituary. But *I* will respond by saying that if a horrific violent crime is committed, and race, financial status, mistakes, and bias play *no* role in the conviction, then I have absolutely no moral problem with the death penalty. The only problem I have with it is that it is *too* humane. In this country, the person is usually put to death by lethal injection. They feel the same amount of "pain and suffering" that one feels when they are anesthetized before an operation. And as for the issue of *deterrence,* it might not deter a future perpetrator from committing crimes again, but putting a guilty murderer to death guarantees that *that* murderer could never escape from prison, be paroled, and commit future crimes. For argument's sake, I am referring to those criminals that we know, with 100% certainty, committed the crimes they were charged with.[11] The family of the victims have to live with the pain and suffering of losing a loved one for the rest of their lives. The criminal gets to go to sleep early.

To return to the topic discussed in a previous chapter…can someone explain to me why a person who is against the death penalty has no problem with the killing of animals — such as when they go fishing or hunting for sport, and not for food — and small insects who pose no threat? I have no problem, however, with killing animals that can hurt us. Mosquitoes suck your blood and can transmit diseases, such as malaria and yellow fever. Flies hang around in shit and then land on your food while you're eating at home or in a restaurant.[12]

Just because we are physically bigger than ants, why does that give us moral superiority over them? Personally, I think that Sadaam Hussein, Osama bin Laden, Hitler, and people who rape, sodomize, and murder children are infinitely inferior not only to insects, but to pieces of shit. And to those who would argue that it's okay to kill animals, because they are a "lower form of life" than humans, *I* would argue that that is precisely what the "people" I just mentioned *are*...even though they might *look* like human beings.

CHAPTER 8

The Road To Forgiveness

Forgiveness has long been considered a virtue. Religions, as well as self-help books, preach that it is high-minded to "let go" of all the anger we feel toward a person who has done us wrong. The image of the crucifixion of Jesus Christ is the fountainhead of this concept.

People have been known to forgive the murderer of their child. After holding on to feelings of anger, hatred, and wanting revenge, the "letting go" of these feelings removed an enormous weight they had been carrying around. It was an emotional catharsis; a passageway to freedom. If one hangs on to their hate, it is argued, he is allowing the wrongdoer to *continue* to victimize him. If the person hates you as much as you hate him, he would be only too happy to know that your hatred is immobilizing you, contributing to your high blood pressure, and putting you at a greater risk of having a stroke or heart attack.

I agree that we should not allow someone to immobilize us long after the offense was committed. But does this always mean we should forgive the person? As with loving everyone indiscriminately, does this not cheapen the whole concept of forgiveness?

There have been examples of people who have committed terrible crimes, who later became truly sorry for what they had done, apologized to their victims and their family members, and asked for forgiveness. There have also been heartwarming examples of their pleas being granted.

What about criminals who *don't* feel remorse, or who even take pleasure in what they have done? Should this same forgiveness be meted out? If one were to answer "No," then the above examples of self-inflicted ailments could be cited as consequences. But does one need to forgive in order to let go?

Several years ago, a black man was tied to a truck, and dragged through the streets to his death. As he was being carted away, the white racist who committed this crime was asked if he had anything to say. "Suck my dick" was his reply. Should a subhuman be granted the same forgiveness as a person who is truly sorry and repentant? I think the answer lies in a statement that the mother of a murder victim said about the murderer. "He's not worth my time; he's not worth my thoughts." She didn't *forgive* him, as he was not deserving of forgiveness. But after a period of grieving, the mother decided that she would no longer allow him to victimize her.

One of my favorite quotes in literature comes from Howard Roark, the hero in Ayn Rand's *The Fountainhead*. His nemesis, Ellsworth Toohey (who has been trying to destroy him in every way) confronts Roark, and invites him to tell Toohey what he thinks of him in any words he wishes. "But I don't think of you," was his perfect response.

One day, in a high school class, I asked one of my classmates a question. She angrily snapped at me. A little later on, she apologized, and said it had nothing to do with me. There had been some issues she had been dealing with. I respected her for apologizing, and considered the slate wiped clean. But there have been incidents in which someone has said a terrible thing to me and never apologized. Even if it happened to me as a young child, I never forgot it, and never wanted anything to do with that person again.

Throughout life, there is always going to be someone who

intensely dislikes you, where the feeling is reciprocal. I have been amongst these people in work situations, and it is very uncomfortable. Some people have advocated that you should greet people, even those you can't stand. Maybe they're right on some level, but somehow, I don't want to give any more than I get. Did you ever greet someone, only to get a barely imperceptible upward nod of their head in response? Some people will smile, and immediately return their face to their original expression. It is just like the "nod," but with another part of their body. Others will give a quick wave, like they're swatting a mosquito away. The recipient of the "greeting" wishes he hadn't gotten one in the first place. Did someone who you saw a lot always look away or look toward the floor when they passed you? It doesn't exactly engender much affection or warmth in me.

An authentic smile, sometimes from a perfect stranger, makes me feel so good. It not only acknowledges my presence, but tells me that my presence gave them pleasure. I love it when people wish me a nice day, and are friendly. I pick up on it, and respond in kind.

Sometimes someone does something bad to you, but it hasn't reached the level of murdering your child. I'm talking about ruthless people who screw people out of money in business deals. Sometimes they will hide behind a friendly and back-slapping exterior, but are merely sharpening their fangs. They believe in winning at all costs, and people's "feelings" are for fairy tales. Robert Ringer talks about these kinds of people in his books, and adopted a very constructive attitude regarding his "teachers" at *Screw U*. Whenever he was screwed over by one of them, he didn't hate them; he hated *himself*. He considered whatever money he lost as the *tuition* he had to pay these "teachers" for the lessons they taught him.

I have read many variations of the application of this philosophy. A man is beaten up by a bully as a youngster. He becomes a great martial artist, and looks for this person years later…not to beat *him* up, but to thank him for inspiring him to get into martial arts.

An obese kid is mercilessly taunted by a particularly cruel classmate, or an obese adult is the recipient of a savage quip from a stranger or a blind date. He resolves right then and there that no one will *ever* be able to say that to him again. He thrusts himself with total immersion into a health and fitness lifestyle.

A homely and scrawny girl with braces and glasses is taunted by her classmates in high school. She goes on to become a world-class bodybuilder and fitness model.

A child is told by a teacher that he will never amount to anything. An "expert" tells an aspiring pianist, singer, or writer that he should quit, because he'll never make it. Like an aikido master, these people "took the force," redirected it, and used it as the motivation for their transcendence.

CHAPTER 9

Freedom And Obscenity

Obscene: 1. offensive to morality and decency; indecent. 2. intended to stimulate sexual appetite or lust; lewd. 3. abominable; disgusting; repulsive. (*Random House Webster's College Dictionary*)

When discussing obscenity, everyone has a different definition as to what it is. Looking up the definition in the dictionary didn't offer much help, because the adjectives used to define it are just as nebulous, indefinable, and as open to interpretation as the word they try to define.

Yet, I am reminded of the famous quote by United States Supreme Court Judge Potter Stewart, in the case *Jacobellis v. Ohio* (1964). "I shall not today attempt further to define the kinds of material I understand to be embraced within that shorthand description ["hard-core pornography"]; and perhaps I could never succeed in intelligently doing so. But *I know it when I see it*, and the motion picture involved in this case is not that."[13] The motion picture he refers to is *The Lovers* (1958). "A showing of the film in Cleveland Heights, Ohio's Coventry Village, resulted in a criminal conviction of the theater manager for public depiction of *obscene* material. He appealed his conviction to the United States Supreme Court, which reversed the conviction and ruled that the film was not obscene in its written opinion (Jacobellis v. Ohio)."[14]

In the same Wikipedia listing that comes up when Googling *The Lovers* (1958), under *I know it when I see it* (page 3 of 4), they go on to write: "This was modified in *Memoirs v. Massachusetts* (1966), in which obscenity was defined as anything patently offensive, appealing to the prurient interest, and of no redeeming social value. Still, however, this left the ultimate decision of what constituted obscenity up to the whim of the courts, and did not provide an easily applicable standard for review by the lower courts. This changed in 1973 with *Miller v. California*. The Miller case established what came to be known as the Miller Standard, which clearly articulated that three criteria must be met for a work to be legitimately subject to state regulations. The Court recognized the inherent risk in legislating what constitutes obscenity, and necessarily limited the scope of the criteria. The criteria were:

1. The average person, applying local community standards, looking at the work in its entirety, appeals to the prurient interest.
2. The work must describe or depict, in an obviously offensive way, sexual conduct or excretory functions.
3. The work as a whole must lack 'serious literary, artistic, political, or scientific values.'"

Another case involved the group U-Live 2. Material that they were performing was accused of being "obscene," and a merchant was prosecuted for continuing to sell their records after a ban was instituted.

This section was really hard to write, because I can't define what it is, myself. However, like Judge Stewart, I know it when I see it. Sometimes, there might be a consensus by the overwhelming majority that certain things are obscene, and a person is prosecuted as a result. But then I think of other things — such as war, violent and white collar crime, and the blatant lies of politicians (which are not prurient, but nevertheless obscene) — and wonder if they might rightly be included in the same classification.

First, I would like to examine the various definitions. The first one listed in the *Random House Webster's College Dictionary* (offensive to morality and decency; indecent) is obviously too broad and ambiguous. What one person may consider immoral or indecent, another might not. Where should the line be drawn? Usually the people that *engage* in what others would define as immoral or indecent behavior do not consider their behavior to be such. The same can be said regarding immoral or indecent *things*. In addition, different countries, cultures, and religions have their own definitions (and as a result, different laws) as to what constitutes obscenity, and the various adjectives used to define it.

The first part of the second definition (intended to stimulate sexual appetite or lust; lewd) is even *harder* to define. To define *lewd* is hard enough, but at least it is easier than defining "intended to stimulate sexual appetite or lust," because *lewd* is a subsection.

If "intended to stimulate sexual appetite or lust" were a definition of *obscene*, then bikinis, beauty pageants, body-building competitions, fitness modeling, colognes, and health clubs could all be classified as obscene. The list could obviously go on and on. Sometimes, in magazines which do *not* display nudity, and are *not* considered "lewd," sex is blatantly used to generate sales. An example of this is magazines that use male models whose crotches are heavily padded, in order to draw the eyes to where the advertisers want them to be…and to sell more underpants. As in movies, television shows, and even the choice of anchorwoman on a news broadcast, sex sells.

As for the third definition (abominable; disgusting; repulsive), the ambiguity is obvious. We have all encountered people who classify others — and the things they do or have done — with the above pejoratives. At the same time, these people and their families do *not*. And when these terms are used, it is often with no reference to sex.

I would now like to examine the definitions listed in Wikipedia. Regarding definition 1, what is an "average" person? Does this mean that if the *majority* of people share a certain view, that it is correct? The Nazis all shared the same view regarding the inferiority of Jews, and all Nazis who believed in and willingly *implemented* Nazi ideology were evil. A Nazi who wasn't "average" might have joined the party because he thought he had no choice, and would otherwise have been killed. But he might have avoided implementing Nazi protocol, and secretly tried to help as many innocent victims as possible.

I don't like the word "average," anyway. Most great achievements in history were accomplished by people who were above "average" in ideals, talent, determination, and vision.

As for definition 2, what constitutes offensive sexual conduct? Does this mean that sexual conduct which is appropriate in one's bedroom may be offensive elsewhere? The word "offensive" also presupposes the question, "Offensive to whom?" People who did *not* hate Jews were offensive to the Nazis; performing oral sex on men in parked cars is *not* offensive to hookers on the street, nor to their johns (some of whom are judges, politicians, doctors, and lawyers). A woman whose body is not completely covered is offensive in Saudi Arabia. Wearing a bikini could be punishable by death.

Kissing could be construed as offensive sexual conduct. There was once a law in Boston that punished kissing in public by life in prison. Some hookers will not kiss on the mouth, because they consider it to be "too personal." Yet we see people kissing on TV all the time, as well as in public. But if a couple were caught having sex in public, they would be arrested.

It would be considered offensive and wrong for a priest or nun to have sex, because they flew down from Heaven. Being abstinent (when they in fact *are*) is how they sacrifice and show their love for God. How giving up something that represents one of the joys of life could be considered a virtue (when they would not even have been here had their parents not had sex) is beyond me. But that is another issue. Maybe a partial reason for all the child molestation that is rampant in the Catholic Church is a result of this repression...a repression designed to suppress a fundamental human need (or maybe more accurately, a need of *most* people).

Regarding "excretory" functions, at least this is now more specific. Eating is not considered offensive, but defecating is...even though the latter is the natural progression of eliminating through one hole that which was taken in through another. But I definitely can relate to excretory functions being offensive. Shit — or the prospect of watching someone shit — grosses me out. And when nature calls me to do what people do, I prefer to do it in total privacy.

As to definition 3, we have all seen movies or read books or magazines which lacked "serious literary, artistic, political, or scientific values" — which were entertaining, but were obviously not obscene. So this definition holds no water at all.

Not listed in the two sets of definitions, but prevalent whenever there is an attempt to define *obscene*, is "has no redeeming social value." This is my favorite. If obscenity were banned based on this definition, we couldn't go bowling, play pool or Bingo (when going to the symphony, ballet, the opera, or to an art museum would be a more "noble," "spiritual," and "intellectual" endeavor), sunbathe at the pool, watch situation comedies, or listen to Howard Stern. We couldn't drink Coke, or attend punk rock, heavy metal, or rap concerts, either.

The Jerry Springer Show and *Professional Wrestling* are absolute shit. They fit definition 3, as well as the "has no redeeming social value" definition to a "t." Obviously, the networks don't consider them to be obscene. Sometimes, when I've needed a good laugh, I've watched them. But I made sure to purify myself afterward with Bach.

Just because I can't precisely define what obscenity is, that does not mean I haven't witnessed it, and does not mean that what I saw or heard was not obscene. Recall the honest admission of Judge Potter Stewart that I quoted earlier. Naturally, how we are raised, our religious beliefs, and culture, all play a role in shaping our attitudes, opinions, and sensibilities. Being raised well does not guarantee that a child will *turn out* well; similarly, growing up under the most challenging conditions does not mean that the child cannot or will not transcend his circumstances.

One day, as a youngster, I witnessed an act of obscenity. I observed a gorgeous woman walking down 13th Avenue in Brooklyn. A boy, possibly in his late teens, became so intimidated by her beauty that he jumped in front of her, pulled down his pants, and proceeded to grab and fondle his testicles and penis. His impotence to win this girl over by charm or intelligence indicated self-hatred, and prompted him to react in the only way he knew how…as the primitive animal that he was. I was so full of revulsion that I remember thinking that had I been a dictator, I would have had him executed.

Sometimes, the situation, location, and context determine whether or not certain behaviors or dress codes are acceptable. Wearing a bikini on the beach is acceptable; in the classroom or office, it is not. A thong is acceptable on the beaches of Rio de Janiero. On Jones Beach, it is not. But nudity is acceptable on nude beaches. Seeing the breasts of an Australian aborigine or African bush woman on public television is "anthropological," but seeing Cindy Crawford's would be "prurient."

Children must not be exposed to "adult" films or books, but it's okay for them to be exposed to the murders that are reported on the six o'clock news, and it's okay to buy Junior a toy gun for his birthday. When he sees me, he can aim it at me, and shout, "Bang! Bang! You're dead." If it had been a *real* gun (which this is preparation for…like his sister's training bra is preparation for the real thing), then I *would* have been dead. It is acceptable for a woman to go topless or nude on a nude beach, but it's illegal for her to go topless in Central Park (even if she's flat-chested). It's legal for a man to do so, however, even if he suffers from gynecomasia (and has larger breasts than a flat-chested woman). It's also legal to breast-feed an infant in public (but not an adult).

CHAPTER 10

Dealing With Irrationality

I consider myself to be a pretty laid-back guy, and I truly try to treat others the way I like to be treated. But I admit that the hate, rage, and irrationality I witness on a regular basis really throw me for a loop. Perhaps the place I witness this behavior the most is behind the wheel of a car.

In this day and age, unless one lives on a remote island, or in a place with an extremely small population (and they don't venture far away), it is almost impossible never to have encountered the wrath of another driver. I guarantee that if you ask *anyone* who drives regularly (especially in a big, crowded city), each and every person will have encountered a driver who gave them the finger, cursed them, and sat on the horn when they wanted to get into a left lane to make a turn coming up soon…but weren't immediately allowed to do so.

I have been given the finger, called every obscenity in the book, been honked at, and tailgated, even when I was driving above the speed limit. I have had drivers who motioned for me to pull onto the shoulder of the highway (so they could assault me), because I pulled in front of them onto the highway from the entrance ramp too slowly. I have had drivers go into a rage when I accelerated too slowly for them from a red light, or didn't move quickly enough when the light turned green. I have had drivers sit on the horn at my tail when I have been lost, and was looking for a house number on a lonely country road at night.

I have witnessed car chases in the city, and I have incurred the wrath of people who thought I was trying to steal their parking space, when I innocently thought they were double parked in front of the spot. I have had drivers yell at me when *they* were the ones going the wrong way down a one-way street. The list goes on and on.

Some people say that driving brings out the worst in people, and transforms some of them into wild animals. I disagree. They already *are*. Driving is merely the catalyst that fans the flames of their hate and rage. I admit that I am affected by these people. I *hate* rude people, and feel the need to "explain" things to irrational people… which is pretty irrational *itself*, especially when you're driving. And even if you *did* prove to someone that they were wrong, just as the people whose shit doesn't stink, how many people would ever admit it? Maybe if you were having a calm, intelligent conversation with someone, they would. But you cannot hold one when you're driving. There are so many other things to think about. And if you react with anger to someone — even if he is 100% wrong — you can get shot or have your car rammed, for the purpose of forcing you to get out of your car. Then, you can be assaulted. At the least, you're most likely to get off with a "Fuck you, asshole!"

I am wrong for letting people like this ruin my day, and often remember the specific incidents many years later. The solution (although easier said than done)? You don't have to be "right," only safe. Chances are, you will never see that person again. You will see others like that, but it is not likely to be that particular individual. You don't have to "explain" anything to anyone. First of all, there isn't time. When the light changes, they will drive away in mid-sentence. Even if you *were* right (and they knew it), if you react angrily to someone else, they will almost never admit that they were in the wrong. It's a face-saving thing. In addition, if you are an intelligent, rational, and confident person with a lot of self-respect, you would not have the *need* to prove you're right. The mutterings of a random piece of shit on the street — who has zero importance and significance (especially to *your* life) — should be of no greater significance than a dog barking at you.

I once had a martial arts instructor whom I interviewed. I decided that even if I couldn't find a magazine to publish the interview, I would get to pick the brain of a martial artist in terms of the application of the philosophy of a true martial artist to everyday life situations. One of my questions was: "Ed Parker believed that physical force should only be used as a last resort, such as in saving your life, or the life of a loved one. In all other situations, such as someone screaming obscenities at you, can you always maintain the attitude, 'As long as he doesn't touch me…'?" His answer was "Yes. Name-calling is not going to harm me; that's their problem. If that's what their feelings are, and they have to prove themselves, so be it. It's not worth my time or effort to get into a shouting match and use my energy to go back and forth with obscenities. In today's society, why instigate a situation? It's better to just turn the other way, go about my business, and just walk. They're not harming me; that's *their* situation, *their* problem. Life is too short. That's not to say there aren't times when I'm driving my car, for example, and I feel rage and anger coming up. But then I have to sit back and say, 'Wait a second. Where is this coming from?' It usually is coming from another situation that had happened that day or the day before, that I kept inside of me and had not let out during my training. But in relation to the person screaming obscenities at me…I don't need to go into *them*. That's like trying to fuel the fire; I want to put it out. The best way to put it out is to just ignore the situation. The best fighter is a person who never gets *into* a fight; you never lose."[15]

The other thing that one can do to *not* be affected by the lice of the world is to be the best you can possibly be. If you work out, and eat a healthy diet, chances are your appearance will be improved. Most people are overweight, so the next time a person curses you while driving or is rude to you in everyday life, be glad you look like you do, and that they look like they do. Although an adversary will rarely admit it, they know if you are better-looking than they are. If the person smokes, be happy that they do, and you don't. And since rage can expedite or cause heart attacks and strokes, when you refuse to allow an irrational person to affect you, you have *won* the confrontation. Bad and/or irrational people are not significant enough for you to be affected by what they say…unless you have a major problem with self-esteem. They are not *worth* your thoughts. As long as they don't touch you, anything else is just hot air.

Become financially successful by the proper use of your mind, talents, and rationality. Knowing that almost everyone in the world (and his brother) wants to be rich — and to make more money if they *are* — be happy that you have something that someone else wants, but can't have.

Use humor to defuse your anger. Imagine that the person who is calling you a fucking asshole is a high-level priest, and laugh at the incongruity of his supposed "status" and "goodness."

Have you ever gotten a parking or speeding ticket? Welcome to the club. When David Letterman gets a speeding ticket, it is simply more fodder for his jokes. Unless it is a situation where he is hauled into court or has his license suspended for repeated infractions, the money Letterman or LeBron James has to pay is the equivalent of a nickel to most people.

And the next time you get a parking ticket, put it in perspective, and think of the kind of person who could actually earn his or her *living* giving out parking tickets. To a rich person, a ticket is like a mosquito bite…a minor nuisance…as are meter maids. But they do what they do, because that kind of work is most likely all they *can* do. And if they *can* do better, what does it say about a person who would choose to do that shit?

Put it in perspective. There are people who *create*, and achieve great things in life…whether in science, medicine, technology, music, art, or literature…and there are people who earn their living doling out pain.

What about speeding tickets? Isn't it dangerous to drive too fast?

Sometimes it is (depending on what the term "too fast" means). Occasionally, on a straight, open highway out West in the desert, I think it is unsafe *not* to drive faster. The faster you reach your destination, the less likely it will be that you'll get drowsy and fall asleep behind the wheel. I've seen speed limits go up by 10 mph on the same highway, when no improvements had been made. The road did not automatically get instantly safer, but the people who wouldn't be getting tickets now, had been getting tickets for driving the same speed.

Policemen and state troopers exert a lot of power. They can stop you and mete out punishment, but you cannot do the same. If you're stopped, be respectful, polite, and calm, but don't suck up to them, either. Do not allow another person to make you lose your dignity and act in a less than respectful manner to *yourself*. And if you want to limit the encounters you have with the authorities, be ever-conscious of the speed limits....not to drive more slowly because it is always safer to do so, but to avoid the forfeiture of money, as well as inconvenience, unpleasantness, and the possible humiliation you will encounter if you are stopped.

What about people who say that there *has* to be a line drawn somewhere, and that if you go above the speed limit, you should get a ticket? Well, if a couple with "Just Married" fliers on their car are driving one mph above the speed limit, and a cop gives them a ticket, I would consider that cop to be nothing more than a piece of shit. I would say the same regarding cops who would detain a person so as to give him a ticket, even in a situation where there is a verifiable emergency (as when one is rushing to the hospital to see a dying parent). These situations *have* happened.

Sometimes Good Samaritans do good deeds and are punished for them. When someone does something kind for another person *anonymously*, that is indicative of a truly fine person…as they are not doing what they are doing to receive any credit for it, but only because they take pleasure in doing the right thing and helping people. An example is people who feed the meters next to the cars of complete strangers. I think this is a beautiful and heartwarming act. But I have also heard of a policeman asking such a person if the car was his. When the policeman was told it wasn't, the Good Samaritan received a citation. I would consider such a policeman to be the same thing as the one who gives a speeding ticket to married couples going one mph above the speed limit, and who insists on detaining and ticketing a person in an emergency situation.

CHAPTER 11

Racism

R acism: A belief or doctrine that inherent differences among the various human races determine cultural or individual achievement, usu. involving the idea that one's own race is superior. (*Random House Webster's College Dictionary*)

While many people do not believe that differences among the various races determine cultural or individual achievement, or that one's own race is superior, there nevertheless *are* differences. I can almost always tell when I am speaking with a black person on the phone, just as I can recognize an Irish, British, or Hispanic accent. People's racial and cultural heritages determine certain behaviors and attitudes. Different cultures have different styles of food, social customs, music, and art. So according to the above definition, if we take out the part about "usu. involving the idea that one's own race is superior," a person would not be classified as a racist if he believed merely that there are inherent differences.

Many people *are* racist by definition, but almost no one will ever admit that *they* are...especially a politician. For a celebrity, famous athlete, or a politician to be caught with his "pants down" or their "hands in the cookie jar" in terms of uttering something indiscreet regarding race is a potentially career-ending proposition...necessitating a massive spin campaign. On April 6, 1987, Al Campanis, the former Dodgers vice president, appeared on *Nightline* with Ted Koppel. His career was ruined when he said that blacks may not have some of the necessities to manage [a major league baseball team]. On April 4, 2007, on MSNBC's *Imus in the Morning,* Don Imus referred to the black members of the Rutgers women's basketball team as "nappy-headed hos." All Hell broke loose, and he ended up going to black "leader" Al Sharpton, the one man who could validate his mea culpa. He was hoping the incident could be put behind him, and he'd go back to work again. The rendezvous with a true racist and race agitator did not work (although Don Imus is currently back on the air). I remember wondering what *white* leader a black person would go to if he wanted to spin out of an indiscreet racial reference he or she made about a white person. No one came to mind.

People love statistics, but when it is pointed out that the overwhelming majority of black people score less than whites on standardized IQ tests, it indicates "racism." The explanation of the disparity is that the majority of blacks come from a completely different socioeconomic background with different life circumstances, such as: a broken home with a single parent; a parent or parents who were alcoholics or drug addicts; a parent who was never home, because he or she was the sole breadwinner (and had to work more than one job to make ends meet); the proliferation of gangs and violence in their neighborhoods). All these things *can* be a partial explanation as to why a person's upbringing and their environmental circumstances would not be the ideal set of circumstances conducive to obtaining a high score on an IQ test. And yes…it *has* been pointed out that there should be a much broader barometer of measuring intelligence, ability, talent, and capacity than the standardized IQ tests measure). But regardless of the reasons, blacks *do* score lower on these tests. When it is pointed out by a white person, that person has, of course, opened himself up to being called a racist.

But if that same person observes that the majority of the greatest professional basketball players have been black, that's okay. It is "indiscreet" or "racist" to point out differences in IQ tests, athletic ability, or the fact that statistically, blacks commit more violent crime than whites do, but totally okay to celebrate a Puerto Rican Day Festival, as well as the diversities in the food, art, and music of different countries and cultures. Imagine someone saying he likes Italian food, and being called a racist, because he doesn't enjoy other kinds of food as much. I have no interest in *soul food*, so that must make me a racist. But I love Cuban, Thai, Japanese, and Indonesian food…so maybe I'm only *partially* racist…even though I feel that my taste buds don't give me much of a say in the matter.

In the world of classical music, the greatest composers have been white. This is not opinion, but fact. Bach, Mozart, Beethoven, Schubert, Schumann, Brahms, Liszt, Chopin, Debussy, Ravel, Rachmaninoff, etc. have written masterpieces which are the staples of the repertoire of classical instrumentalists and orchestras. If a classical musician did not perform a composition by a single black composer, he could still have a highly successful career. To say a musician loves or specializes in the Viennese, German, French, or Russian repertoire is entirely proper (even though these are designations of national origin). There have been concerts and recordings celebrating the music of black composers. However, if a classical performer said he was going to give a concert of music by white composers, it would sound absurd, if not "racist." Similarly, there has been *Black News*, as well as programs celebrating the black experience on TV. There have been Miss Black America beauty pageants, as well. But there has never been *White News* and Miss White America.

Why have there not been more celebrated black composers in the realm of classical music? Part of the explanation is that they did not have this art form available to them, and were not exposed to it. The fact that George Walker, William Grant Still, and Samuel Coleridge-Taylor are highly respected classical composers indicates that "race" does not hold a monopoly on art. If more blacks had been brought up in the same environment, and had the same exposure to classical music as the previously mentioned composers, there would undoubtedly have been more black composers who made it into the standard repertoire of all performing classical musicians.

More and more black classical performers are joining the ranks of orchestras, are conducting, and are performing as soloists. The late great Marion Anderson has always been celebrated for her great talent, as well as for her dignity. The fact that she endured racial discrimination, and was a pioneer, inspired and paved the way for future generations of black musicians in the same way that Jackie Robinson did for athletes. Leontyne Price, William Warfield, Isaiah Jackson, and André Watts are examples of highly celebrated black classical musicians.

In the realm of jazz piano, Art Tatum and Oscar Peterson have always been my heroes, and I loved the great singer Sarah Vaughan. My life has also been richer because of the music of Stevie Wonder, Al Jarreau, George Benson, and Anita Baker.

If we can celebrate the music, art, cuisine, and culture of the various ethnic groups, why can't we acknowledge the inherent differences in the vernacular, and mannerisms? In the same manner that Al Hirschfeld took a prominent feature of a celebrity and drew a caricature of him, great impressionists like Rich Little, David Frye, and Frank Caliendo mimicked the voices and mannerisms of the people they portrayed. Few white comedians could get away with racial humor, but Don Rickles is an example of one that *could*. During a celebrity roast, he was going down the line insulting the people on the dais. When he got to a black lady (was it LaWanda Page?), he said, "LaWanda…only the windows!" I thought it was hilarious. One of the ways we can break down prejudices and come together is to laugh at perceived stereotypes. Incidentally…I have heard that in real life, Don Rickles is not at all like the person he portrays in his act.

In one of his acts, Eddie Murphy imitates Italians reacting to seeing *Rocky*. Notwithstanding the fact that I would be accused of being a "racist" if I imitated blacks in a comedy act, I loved the performance. He really had the voice and mannerisms down to a "t."

∾

A college sociology class was once divided into groups. Each group had about an equal number of blacks and whites in it. They convened to various corners of the classroom to discuss whether or not there were inherent racial differences between blacks and whites. Various topics, such as soul food, rap, and break dancing came up. Most of the students agreed that these things were endemic to the black experience and culture. One of the white participants brought up the fact that some of the black vernacular was uniquely their own. In fact, there had been talk of making Ebonics a language. For example, "bad" means "good," as in "I'm the *baddest* man on the planet." "Diss" means "disrespecting someone." One student pointed out a phrase that blacks say all the time: "Ya know what I'm sayin'?"

One of the black students asked a white student (who hadn't spoken yet) if *he* had noticed any differences in the vernacular. He said that he *had*, but didn't really want to talk about it. "Oh, come on," said the black student. "That's what we're here for."

"Well, all right," he said." I've noticed that blacks say the word 'motherfucker' an awful lot."

With that, the black student started to become angry. It really struck a nerve.

"So *that's* your stereotype of black people, huh," he said. "We love, we produce, we struggle, we become doctors, lawyers, talk show hosts, even though *your* ancestors tried to enslave us…and *that's* the only thing that comes to mind when you think of black people."

"Hey, chill out, man!" another white student chimed in. "You asked him a question, and he answered you. He didn't say that there weren't blacks who haven't done great things, made extraordinary contributions, and weren't great people. He said he noticed that they said that word a lot. And if you want *my* honest observation, they *do* say that word a lot."

"Well," screamed the black student, "that just shows what a motherfucking racist you are!"

Many of the Olympians say they want to win a gold medal for their "country." Indeed, there was a daily tally in the recent 2012 Olympics, comparing how many gold, silver, and bronze medals each participating country won. Why do we celebrate the "superiority" of some countries who win more medals or gold medals than other countries? Why does this national "pride" rub off on his or her fellow countrymen, who didn't compete at all...but just so happen to have been born in the same country? Are they superior by *association*?

Why has there not been an Olympics in which blacks competed against whites? Because that would be considered "racist." But aren't people from different countries of a different race? If not, why is national origin a characterization, when *color of skin* is not? Why not have an Olympics where everyone competed for their own ass — and glory — rather than for that of a country? And in the instances of team sports, why not have Russians, Chinese, Americans, etc. on the same team competing against other teams of an equally diverse national makeup?

If blacks are not less intelligent than whites, then why do they accept the benefits of affirmative action? In *Outliers*, Malcolm Gladwell cites a study that tracked the future success of blacks admitted to The University of Michigan law school. Blacks that were given the benefit of affirmative action performed just as well as their higher-scoring white counterparts when they got into the work force. This was because even though their scores were lower, they (their scores) were *good enough*. That may be true, but the point is that affirmative action is not only obscene, but blatantly racist. It is just as obscene as being drafted — or volunteering — to go to war and die for your country without being allowed to vote. If I were a black person, I would be totally insulted to have this even offered to me.

And for anyone who would welcome it, their acceptance indicates that they want to have their cake and eat it, too. They don't like being considered less intelligent, but will accept having the playing field tilted in their favor, as well as the benefits. For a white person with superior grades to be rejected by a college in favor of a black person with lesser grades — to "level the playing field" and/or to make up for the sins of our ancestors — is a grave injustice. And it is an equal injustice to the brilliant black people who can score higher than blacks *and* whites *without* any preferential treatment.

Would it be ethical for a white family to sell their house to a white family with identical income and down payment in favor of a black family? Yes. The issue is individual *property rights*, not race. Secondly, how could it ever be proved that selling to the white family was racially motivated? It might have been, but if two families have identical incomes and down payments, how can it be considered *wrong* or *illegal* for the owners to choose who they wanted to buy their home? Maybe the white family did not consider the black family to be nice people, and maybe the white family impressed them with their warmth and friendliness, and established a kind of bond through mutual interests.

But even if the sale *was* racially motivated…again, the issue is not of race, but of individual property rights…i.e., the right to do with *your* property whatever you want to. And no...they are *not* infringing on the black family's rights, because they (the black family) have a right to buy a house somewhere else, to whomever wants to sell one to them. And when *they* have a house and want to sell it, they, in turn, have the right to *not* sell it to a white family if they don't want to.

I can anticipate the arguments that in the recent past, blacks could not live in neighborhoods where they wanted to, and that they were barred from the upper levels of certain industries. It took the pioneer Jackie Robinson to break the color barrier in baseball when he joined the Brooklyn Dodgers in 1947. Is our system now perfect? No. But today, blacks have achieved staggering professional and financial success. It might be argued that the list is not as long as it should be, but it is a long one, nonetheless. A *partial* list would include: Oprah Winfrey, Tiger Woods, Michael Jordan, LeBron James, Kobe Bryant, Magic Johnson, Floyd "Money" Mayweather, P. Diddy, Chris Rock, and Denzel Washington. Perhaps the greatest example of all is Barack Obama. John McCain, the man he defeated for the presidency, said in his concession speech that he understood how important this was for African-Americans. Indeed, people such as Oprah Winfrey and Jesse Jackson were shown with tears streaming down their faces. Even though this was a great milestone for them, it's too bad that *competency* did not come with the package. His abysmal presidency — and his re-election — should cause tears, but not of joy.

Blacks *and* whites say there should be more blacks in front office and managerial positions (in sports and in other professions). That would be nice, but the color of one's skin should never be the arbiter of who gets hired for a certain position. It should be based *only* on merit, qualifications, or — as in the example of property rights — on whom the owner of a particular private company or organization *wants* to hire.

In the case of a *publicly* owned company, if a black person is more qualified for an available position than a white person, then the black person should definitely get the job. But the black person should not get the job solely because whites greatly outnumber blacks in that particular line of work, or because of a quota system. This means that if 99% of the employees at a given company are white, and a position becomes available, a white applicant should be chosen over a black applicant if he is more qualified for the position. Many people, including whites, would say that the black person should be hired...yet find nothing wrong with the fact that the over-whelming majority of basketball players in the NBA are black. And there *is* nothing wrong with that...as long as the particular black players at a given time are more qualified than the white players who are vying for the same position.

The members of the Black Panthers would have a right to deny me admission into their private organization, assuming I wanted to become a member. And if I were an actor interested in portraying a black person in a film, it would not be morally wrong for the direc-tor to choose a black actor in favor of me...even if I were just as fine an actor, with equal credentials.

The above two examples will be construed as very stupid argu-ments, but as for the latter, James Whitmore, in *Black Like Me* (1964) played a white reporter who darkened his skin to experience what it felt like to be black in the segregated South. As for the former, the issue should be one of ideology, not the color of one's skin. Didn't Leonard Bernstein once host the Black Panthers in his home?

If a white person says the word "nigger" (known as the filthiest, ugliest, most offensive word in the English language), he or she is an irredeemable racist. If a white politician used the term freely, his or her career would literally be over…even if a massive spin campaign (referred to earlier) were launched to dig him or herself out of the deep doo-doo. But why is it that when Richard Pryor, Eddie Murphy, and Chris Rock use the term to refer to *themselves*, it's okay? I would think it would be even *worse* to refer to yourself with such a so-called filthy word, because it indicates such a lack of self-respect.

In an effort to prove how *un*prejudiced they are, white people will often refer to white lowlifes as "white trash," but will not use the term "black trash" to refer to the many examples of blacks who totally deserve the epithet. Observe that the overwhelming majority of white people marry white people, and the overwhelming majority of black people marry black people.

Observe people who discriminate against gay people. They are as guilty of prejudice as white people who discriminate against blacks…even though one kind of discrimination is against skin color and racial origin, and the other is against sexual preference. But the word *prejudice* means *pre judge*, and that is precisely what they are doing. Some people make fun of or discriminate against gay people, because it makes them feel more *straight* or macho. Some do it because they are closet gays themselves…as the late Roy Cohn was said to have been. People like these are the worst kind of hypocrites.

Sexual prejudice is another form of racism…not racism by definition, but a subsection. I once took a sociology class, and one of the questions on a multiple choice test was " 'Chris Evert is one of the greatest female tennis players in the world' is an example of a_____."

The "correct" answer was "sexist statement." The correct wording was supposed to have been "Chris Evert is one of the greatest tennis players in the world."

I knew what answer to choose (especially since the professor was a woman) in order to be marked "correct," even though the correct answer was "greatest *female* player." Nothing against the top female tennis players, but however indiscreet it is to point out... there is absolutely no comparison between the number one female and number one male tennis player. If there were, they would be competing against one another. And can someone explain to me why women play only best of three set matches in *all* matches (and receive equal pay) while men play best of five sets in the majors?

It is not *sexist* to point out intrinsic differences between men and women. Statistically, men are stronger physically, but in matters not involving physical strength, I feel that women can compete, and in some instances *surpass* men. I think that even though we don't see many women compete against men in martial arts tournaments, they could match up very well. A top martial artist depends more upon speed and skill than on brute strength. Certainly, in the realm of politics, women compete on an equal footing with men. Women can also perform certain physical maneuvers better than men can, because of their anatomy.

I don't know why there are not more great women chess players, because I certainly feel that many women can equal or surpass many men intellectually. Today, more and more women are getting into math, science, and medicine. In the realm of the performing arts, women compete, and often win, against men at piano and violin competitions. And no, I have no problem with a woman piloting my plane or performing surgery on me. I feel that there is truth in some of the intrinsic personality characteristics — such as *intuition* — that women are supposed to possess in greater capacity than their male counterparts.

CHAPTER 12

Should Drugs
Be Legal?

P eople have been locked away in jail for many years because of the Rockefeller drug laws. If you are caught with heroin or cocaine (especially at an airport), or are caught smuggling large amounts of illegal drugs, you can be jailed, or in some countries, sentenced to death. Should drugs such as cocaine, heroin, and crack be legal? Well, assuming that minors are not affected by it, every competent adult has a right to put into their body whatever they want to, as long as they are not forcing someone else to take it. If they drive, or commit a crime under the influence of a drug or alcohol, that is another issue...because then others *are* affected by their consumption. It can even be argued that a pregnant woman is subjecting an innocent baby to drug addiction. But an adult who willingly takes drugs by himself or with other consenting adults on his own property and in their own homes — and if the drugs are causing no harm to other innocent people — should be allowed to take them.

But these are so harmful to you, it might be argued. True. But why are cigarettes, alcohol, and Big Macs legal? Are not cigarettes and alcohol addictive drugs? Perhaps they kill you more slowly than crack or heroin, but they kill you, nonetheless. People get addicted to, and in some cases, die from prescription drugs, and people slowly get diabetes, as well as get sick and die from an excessive junk food and sugar-laden diet. The aspartame and sucralose in diet sodas are literally poison, the former having been approved because of a political payback.

The issue is freedom and human rights. No one has a right to dictate another's lifestyle, or what their priorities should be. Some people love their cigarettes and junk food so much that they would rather enjoy their lives doing something that gives them so much pleasure than be a health fanatic who lives a long but miserable life. Others, who eat lettuce and seaweed soup and work out at the gym three hours a day, drop dead sooner than their junk-food-eating, cigarette-smoking, obese and sedentary counterparts, because of all the anger, rage, and stress in their lives.[16]

But a smoker does not have a right to smoke around a person who does not smoke, who hates cigarette smoke, and whose health can be affected by second-hand smoke. To those people who do so anyway, even when people ask them not to…I have no sympathy for them when their disgusting habit finally catches up with them. And when someone is smoking outside, where do the butts go when they are finished? They can't go in a garbage can, because they can ignite a fire. They go on the street, or wherever the smoker happens to be standing.

CHAPTER 13

Let's Allow Athletes To Take PEDs

Steroids, human growth hormone, and all kinds of performance-enhancing drugs are now rampant in sports...particularly in baseball and in cycling. Methods to increase oxygen consumption through transfusions of one's own stored blood, and a plethora of means to avoid detection, are endemic to the lives of world-class cyclists. You either "do what everyone else is doing," or you suffer the consequences of being left in the dust by athletes of lesser ability. What is the solution to this problem? The answer is to allow the use of all PEDs across the board. I write this as a person who would never consider taking PEDs under any circumstances. This means that even if I were a professional athlete, and I were instructed to do so by my manager and/or teammates, had zero chance of being caught, and could ensure myself notoriety, endorsements, money, and fame that I would not have achieved had I *not* taken PEDs, I would not do so.

The issue all boils down to the freedom to put into our body anything we want, whether or not "society," the government, or governing bodies condone it. The last time I checked, the government condones aspartame, sucralose, high fructose corn syrup, partially hydrogenated vegetable oil, and McDonald's...all examples of poison. Some items, such as heroin and cocaine, are illegal, yet cigarettes, alcohol, and all kinds of prescription drugs *are* legal. All of the items mentioned can kill you, but because heroin and cocaine can kill you faster than cigarettes and alcohol (assuming someone is not driving under the influence of alcohol and killing themselves or innocent people as a result), the former is illegal, and the latter is legal.

What about the "clean" athlete who is more talented than his PED-taking brethren? Is it fair that a less-talented athlete will now achieve the money, notoriety, and fame that would otherwise have been bestowed upon the superior athlete? How can the playing field be "level"? Well, the "clean" athlete would have the option of taking PEDs, also.

"This would not be fair to the athlete who is concerned with his health and has no desire to put these substances (whether legal or not) into his body," it could be argued. But if we do not own and have the final say over what we may or may not put into our bodies, then we do not have freedom. We have to consider that "rewards" (whether "legitimately" or "illegitimately" achieved) come with a price tag. Is it better to win the Tour de France, the home run title, or the Mr. Universe title, and suffer the physical consequences in the future — by being permanently crippled or dying prematurely — or *not* to take PEDs, not win a contest or title that we otherwise *could* have won — and consequently not achieve the money and fame that go along with it — but live a long and healthy life? Lyle Alzedo, the former football player, and Eldridge Wayne Coleman (aka "Superstar" Billy Graham), the former professional wrestler, are two examples of people who achieved short-term success through their substance abuse, but paid a big price for it later.

It has been argued that in baseball, no amount of PEDs will allow a batter to make better contact with the ball, or improve his eye/hand coordination. "But once contact is made," others would argue, "a given player would not have hit as many home runs as he did. The PEDs bulked him up, gave him more energy, and increased his strength." Because Barry Bonds, and others, were great players *before* they started juicing up, some people believe that we should allow the records and stats achieved through PEDs, as long as they were achieved during the period of legalization.

The problem with all of the above is that — even though there are truths in all the arguments — there is no way to make everything completely fair across the board. Do we throw out all records that were achieved through the help of PEDs after they became illegal? What about the stats that would otherwise *not* have been achieved without PEDs *before* they were banned? Also, how is it verifiable how *much* of an advantage the person achieved? Let us say a home run hitter hits a ball 517 feet and that without PEDs, it would have been 483 feet. The fence was 410 feet away. Does the fact that he would have hit a home run *anyway* carry any weight? What about the situations in which the fences in the outfields of some stadiums were moved in several feet, so as to become more "hitter friendly"? A hitter who was not taking PEDs could have hit home runs that he wouldn't have otherwise.

Does *intention* play a role as to whether or not a PED achieved a better performance? Andy Pettitte admitted to having taken HGH, but said it was to help him recover from injuries, not to increase his performance. But if recovering more quickly enabled him to get on the pitching mound earlier, did this not improve his performance as a baseball player? If he won a game, which he wouldn't have pitched in had he not "recovered" earlier through the use of HGH, this would have affected the outcome of a game.

The point is...even King Solomon would not have been able to devise a system that would completely account for all the differences in performance with or without the use of PEDs. And even if every player who has ever taken PEDs could pinpoint the exact date they started taking them, and how many times they took them, they could not accurately measure the percent of advantage they achieved, or how many times this advantage resulted in their team (in the case of a baseball player) winning a game, or having the score be higher. In the case of a team that lost a game 11-7, when they would have lost 11-10 had certain players taken PEDs, would the fact that they lost anyway weigh less heavily than a team who took the identical amount of PEDs but won the game *because* of it?

What about an athlete who trains very hard, but lives on McDonald's and eats food and drinks liquids with harmful ingredients? What about another athlete who also trains very hard, but eats only organic and unprocessed foods, and supplements with vitamins? All other things being equal, wouldn't the latter athlete have an advantage over the former athlete? Should not some of the harmful substances that the former is putting in his body be deemed illegal?[17] Are steroids more harmful than aspartame in the long run? If so, by how much? Does the athlete who supplements with vitamins have an *unfair* advantage? If so, should vitamins be outlawed? What about the athlete who gained an "unfair" advantage because he innocently ingested a banned substance in a prescription that a doctor gave him for a condition completely unrelated to athletic performance? What about a "clean" athlete who innocently ingested a banned substance that was maliciously put into a food item or drink that the athlete ingested?

I was once on a bicycle trip as a teenager. There were several potheads in the group. At one point, the leader asked one of the kids what he had done with his pot. He said that he put it in the food (that was prepared for our dinner). The look of horror and anger that I displayed prompted some of them to tell me, "Don't worry, nothing will happen to you." Here you have an example of a person who considered the idea of putting mind-altering drugs in his body abhorrent. Yet, had I been an athlete tested for banned substances, I would have been severely punished.

It has been said that PEDs have a big effect on performance, and that their use can help athletes to achieve feats of athleticism that would otherwise not have been deemed possible. But how great are the effects, and by what percentage do they increase athleticism?

If PEDs are banned, then why is it that doctoring a ball—by throwing a "spitball," or by scuffing it—has been considered a slap-on-the-wrist offense? It can get a player thrown out of a game, but—unlike using PEDs—has not kept players out of The Hall of

Fame. Gaylord Perry was elected to The Hall of Fame in 1991, and was the first pitcher to win the Cy Young Award in each league. Not only has he admitted to throwing a "spitball" throughout his career, he even wrote a book about it in 1974 (*Me and the Spitter*). I remember watching Perry on a talk show. Both the interviewer and he were joking and laughing about the "specialty" pitch he employed throughout his career.

1961 Cy Young Award winner Edward Charles "Whitey" Ford was voted into The Hall of Fame in 1974. To quote Wikipedia, "After retiring, Ford admitted in interviews to having occasionally doctored baseballs. Examples were the 'mudball', used at home in Yankee Stadium. Yankee groundskeepers would wet down an area near the catcher's box, where the Yankee catcher Elston Howard was positioned, pretending to lose balance. Howard would put down his hand with the ball and coat one side of the ball with mud, and throw it to Ford. Ford sometimes used the diamond in his wedding ring to gouge the ball, but was eventually caught by an umpire and warned to stop. Howard sharpened a buckle on his shin guard and used it to scuff the ball." The article further says: "Ford admitted doctoring the ball in the 1962 All-Star game at Candlestick Park, to strike out Willie Mays."

As this is being written, the baseball writers have decided not to vote into The Hall of Fame *any* players who became eligible for induction in 2013. Of the players who became eligible, two of them were among the greatest and most dominant ever to play the game. Roger Clemens was a seven-time Cy Young Award winner, and Barry Bonds was a seven-time Most Valuable Player, and eight-time Gold Glove winner.

Records are being broken all the time. But if training methods and use of PEDs are becoming ever more rampant, why is it that humans will *never* run a one-minute mile or a one-hour marathon? Whether or not PEDs are illegal, they — like prostitution — are here to stay.

CHAPTER 14

Do We Own
Our Own Lives?

The topic of euthanasia, or whether or not we have a right to aid in the death of another person or take our *own* life, is a polarizing issue that — like abortion — will always incur heated debate. Everyone is convinced that *they* are right regarding this issue, so even though someone may hold valid arguments against a particular point of view, they will be dismissed. This is especially true for the people who have *religion* on their side.

I believe that Dr. Jack Kevorkian was trying to do the right thing, and was motivated by ending people's suffering. Even if he were acting *illegally,* he was acting in the interests of his patients and their family members. The fundamental issue is *sovereignty* over our own lives. People who do not know the people who were euthanized, and cannot feel their pain, nevertheless feel that they have the right to be moral policemen. They invoke God, saying He should be the sole arbiter of when it is someone's time to go. Yet some of these same people will allow a loved one to remain *technically* alive by being hooked up to a machine. Are *they* not playing God by artificially prolonging a life which would otherwise have ended naturally?

People should not define what someone *else's* definition of "quality of life" should be. For someone to choose euthanasia, or give explicit instructions to his or her family that they want to be put to rest when they reach a specific level of illness, does *not* mean that this person does not want to live, and did not celebrate life during their healthy years. It means that they are past the stage of reasonably hoping for a recovery, they do not want to suffer any more, they do not want to be a physical and emotional burden to their families, and they want to die with the dignity with which they lived.

The precise definition of what that term means, and the precise time or threshold of suffering to be reached before it is time to "let go," will differ between people. So how does one know when the proper time is? The answer is: "The time that is proper for that particular individual and his family, based on his or her wishes at the time, or expressed in words or writing before the individual became debilitated and could not verbally express his or her wishes at a given stage of infirmity."

It should be noted that many people who were euthanized, or *wish* to be at a specified stage, lived wonderful, happy, and productive lives. They want to go out with these feelings and memories still fresh in their minds...*not* to have the final memories of their lives be those of pain, incapacity, and helplessness. If one were to have a "perfect" meal at a world-class five-star restaurant, where the food, service, and experience were so elegant and special that it was something they would always remember...and then go out to McDonald's for dessert, they would have thoroughly corrupted the experience.

What about someone in the throes of paralyzing depression, emotional turmoil, grief, or extreme distress? If anyone has read William Styron's book *Darkness Visible: A Memoir of Madness*, they know that emotional anguish can be even *more* painful than any *physical* pain you could imagine. With medication, therapy — and with time — depression, grief, and pain can subside or even be eliminated. But how does one reconcile the right of sovereignty over one's own life with preventing a person from taking his life when emotional pain becomes too much to bear?

It may seem contradictory, but I would do everything in my power to prevent a person (especially one I loved or cared about) from committing suicide. Someone suffering from cataclysmic depression is temporarily insane...meaning that they can't think rationally. Their only focus is on ending their suffering. This is analogous to "normal" people who suddenly snap and kill a family member during a time of insanity.

When a family member has just been murdered or killed by a drunk driver, or when the wife you are madly in love with suddenly announces that she wants a divorce, at the time, one cannot imagine that he will ever be able to get over the agony. The person is too "close" to the situation. He doesn't have the benefit of hindsight, and cannot believe that time will dissipate the suffering. But he doesn't *have* time. That is why at a time such as this, he needs *compassion*.

All people are different, and will disagree about things. We are individuals who bring to the table different contexts, upbringings, and life experiences. No two people — even married couples — will have identical beliefs, interests, or talents — nor should they. Having a clone would be too boring.

The Palestinian/Israeli conflict will always be, and will never be resolved. Nor will the debate over abortion. This is not being pessimistic, just *realistic*. This is because people *do* think in black and white on various issues, and are totally convinced of the rectitude of their position. You cannot compromise by cutting a baby in half, as King Solomon wisely proposed in order to determine the real mother of a child. And when you invoke God, and have *Him* on your side, you can be even *more* steadfast in your positions. When it comes to preventing the killing of innocent people, sadly, sometimes targeted assassinations — such as those carried out by the Israelis against terrorists intent upon destroying them — are the *only* answer.

Of course, it is too simplistic, idealistic, and irrationally optimistic, but if everyone lived by the oft-repeated cliché, and treated others the way they would like to be treated, a lot of pain and suffering would be ameliorated right off the bat.

CHAPTER 15

Cannibalism: An Appetizing Perspective

C annibalism: 1. the eating of human flesh by another human being, esp. for magical or religious purposes, as to acquire the power of a person killed. 2. the eating of flesh by another animal of its own kind (*Random House Webster's College Dictionary*)

(From *Canibales*, the Spanish name for the Carib people, a West Indies tribe formerly well known for their practice of cannibalism) is the act or practice of humans eating the flesh or internal organs of other human beings *(Wikipedia: The Free Encyclopedia)*

Cannibalism has been around for a long time, and Wikipedia cites the Korowa as a tribe "still believed to eat human flesh as a cultural practice." They cite two kinds of cannibalism: *homicidal cannibalism* (in which the person is killed specifically in order to be eaten) and *necro-cannabalism* (in which the person is already dead, and the remains are eaten).

I really hesitated about including this section in my book. Cannibalism summons images of Hannibal Lecter, whom Anthony Hopkins portrayed so brilliantly in his Academy Award-winning performance in *The Silence of the Lambs* (1991). It also summons images of the evil monster and *real-life* cannibal Jeffrey Dahmer. The purpose of this section is to examine the issue, and determine if, in fact, cannibalism might be a positive thing under certain circumstances.

One of the definitions cited above is the eating of flesh by another animal of its own kind. Even though I spoke about the pain animals feel when they are eaten, and the terror they feel when they know they are about to die,[18] the killing of animals by other animals for food is not considered to be evil. Like a hurricane, tornado, tsunami, or earthquake, it is considered to be a law of nature. When an animal tracks and eats another animal, it isn't considered to be doing so out of maliciousness or evil, but for survival. In the first chapter, I discuss how various animals are anatomically constructed so as to catch food and to survive. Some eat members of a different species, and some eat the flesh of their own kind (one of the above definitions of cannibalism).

But when people think of eating other people, the very idea elicits feelings of depravity, ghoulishness, and revulsion. But some of the survivors of Uruguayan Air Force Flight 571 ate the bodies of dead passengers when their plane crashed in the Andes on October 13, 1972, and they were stranded on top of a mountain for seventy-two days. The ordeal is recounted in several books, films, and documentaries. If the passengers who were eaten were already dead, and eating them represented the difference between death and survival for the remaining passengers (some of whom survived precisely *because* they ate the flesh of other people), then most people would not consider what they did to be wrong.

In order for the people to have survived, the flesh would have had to have nutritional value. Wikipedia (under *Cannibalism*) recounts that "Prior to 1931, *New York Times* reporter William Buehler Seabrook, allegedly in the interests of research, obtained from a hospital intern at the Sorbonne a chunk of human meat from the body of a healthy human killed in an accident, then cooked and ate it. 'It was like good, fully developed veal,' he said."

If some people are *not* "a higher form of life" than animals (which I argue earlier), what would be wrong with eating the flesh of other humans, even if it were not a situation in which *any* food would have to be eaten in order to survive (such as in the case of the Uruguayan plane crash)? Do we not donate our organs after we die, so that others may reap the benefits of our eyes, heart, and liver?

Why not use the flesh of humans to alleviate hunger in destitute countries, where there *is* an emergency situation…where hundreds of children die every day due to malnutrition and starvation? Could not the corpse of an evil criminal be put to good use in that capacity? I have already written that I don't consider some humans to be intrinsically superior to animals, but if the reader does, I could then argue that it is not at all wrong to kill a vicious serial killer and mass murderer, because they *are*, in fact, animals (in the vernacular). They may *look* like a human being, but their primitiveness puts them at the *level* of an animal.

When an evil murderer is put to death, why not offer his flesh to his victims' loved ones… assuming they would not be revolted by the prospect of eviscerating and consuming the contents of the corpse? Some might consider it a "catharsis," however. By devouring the remains of a monster, they can more easily achieve closure… especially when they later go to the toilet to purge the aftermath of the meal from their bodies.

Restaurants might offer the flesh of humans as part of their menu, and chefs could learn the intricacies of the preparation of human cuisine. Cookbooks might soon follow. A restaurant menu item might include "sautéed rack of murderer ass with morels and artichokes," prepared medium rare. And instead of matzoh balls in soup, testicles could be used.

CHAPTER 16

Love, Sex,
And Marriage

Commenting on government wasteful spending, a politician once cited — on a television program — a study that purported to define what love was. He said that if an answer had been determined, he wouldn't want to know. In other words, "If you have to analyze whether or not you're in love with someone, you're not." In the realm of love, specifically *romantic* love, you know it when you feel it. You can specify certain qualities that attract you to the person you love, but the same qualities might be present in people that you *don't* love or don't feel romantic love for.

WHAT KINDS OF LOVE ARE THERE?

There are many kinds. There is the romantic/sexual love we feel for our lover; we feel an equally powerful love for our parents, although sexual feelings are usually not involved. We may say we love a certain musician, writer, artist, or athlete without loving the actual person. We are referring to their accomplishments. A mother may love a son, but not always because of who the son is, but because of the blood relationship and of being involved in the child's struggles since birth.

Love evokes images of a couple holding hands on the beach at sunset, dancing cheek to cheek, kissing, wedding gowns, and children (a "product" of the love). Although love can be defined as the state of having an extreme attraction for a person, a thing, an activity, or an occurrence, I wish to confine my discussion to *romantic* love (i.e., the blissful union between a man and a woman).[19]

Ayn Rand viewed love as a response to one's highest values in another person, with sex representing the ultimate celebration. This is a wonderful, albeit circumscribed, definition. Although the sharing of similar values is an important component of a successful union, it doesn't have to be the *only* one.

When a man and a woman meet, one very often hears the word "vibes" or "chemistry," as an explanation of whether or not there was an attraction. These words are used in an attempt to define the indefinable. It has been said that music begins where words end. It is a realm of expression that ventures *between* the lines, and renders emotion that we can feel and understand, even if we can't verbalize it. In that respect, it is analogous to love. No formulas or listed criteria need be used. We *are* utilizing criteria, but our own personal "vibes" computer spits out the information to us instantly: "That beautiful blonde woman (my instant subjective evaluation) sitting near the couch by the window attracts me." If the attraction is mutual, the relationship can develop into love at various rates of speed...depending on other factors.

In *The Passion of Ayn Rand*, Barbara Branden describes how Ayn Rand met her husband, Frank O'Connor. She saw an actor on a streetcar that was taking them both to a movie set. He had "her kind of face." After pondering for several days how she could get to meet him, she finally decided to step in front of him, and stick her foot out. For them to have been happily married for so many years indicates that they must have embodied each other's highest values. But doesn't this anecdote indicate that Rand's initial attraction was physically motivated? Didn't Frank O'Connor's physical appearance and presence elicit the proper vibes in Ayn Rand?

IS THERE SUCH A THING AS LOVE AT FIRST SIGHT?

There is definitely such a thing as infatuation at first sight. As for *love* at first sight, it depends on what one's definition of love is.

Even though an initial attraction might be based solely on appearance, one's "looks" provide an accurate barometer of whether or not the observer wants to discover what lies beneath the surface of the pulchritudinous façade. The voice, ease and comfort of conversation, similarity of interests, having things in common, and the sharing of core values are other factors that may lead a man and a woman to conclude that they're "in love."[20] Whether or not this is genuine will take time to determine. If, three weeks into the relationship, the woman finds out that the man is an embezzler and a con artist, her love for him may die (assuming that these qualities are not ones she values in a man).

Needless to say, love can grow; a couple meets, they don't love one another, but they do like one another. Gradually, as they share and grow together, and as they learn more pleasing things about one another, the *like* starts to turn into love (although you can love someone and not like them).

Sometimes, certain intangibles come into play. A man might prefer to meet a woman who lives in Manhattan, because it is the cultural and financial hub of New York, as opposed to, say, Brooklyn. He views Manhattan as a place where more is *happening* than in the other boroughs. He meets a woman, and the fact that she lives in Manhattan influences the way he feels about her; his impression of her is intertwined with the financial and cultural perceptions he has of Manhattan. She might even seem more "professional" to him, because she works in a beautiful office in a Manhattan skyscraper, rather than in Brooklyn.

For the same reason that romantic music, champagne, and beautiful surroundings and scenery can enhance an intimate evening, the fact that a man met a woman at a cocktail party in a penthouse can amplify his initial attraction. When Bill met Debra, it was at a black-tie affair with soft mellow jazz playing in the background. To this day, whenever he hears this music, he thinks of Debra.

As he gazed at her, the music, the dazzling view of the city from the seventy-seventh floor, Debra's stunning evening gown, and the elegant surroundings all intertwined with Debra's personality and added to Bill's passion. Had he met her in a slum neighborhood in Brooklyn, he would still have fallen in love with her, but the initial encounter would not have been quite the same. Similarly, he could enjoy making love to her on a New York City subway platform, but the disgusting surroundings would distract from the enjoyment he could have experienced in a less unpleasant environment.

WHAT IS PERSONALITY?

Very often, we hear someone say, "He has no personality." What they really mean is: "He doesn't have a "good" personality," or "His personality is not like mine." Everyone has a personality; the word means: "What kind of a person is he?" "What are the characteristics that define who he is?" Although this is a proper definition, the problem is that everyone has different criteria as to what constitutes a "good" personality.

ARE LOOKS AN ASPECT OF PERSONALITY?

Yes. The package a beautiful person comes in — irrespective of his voice, intelligence, interests, and the sundry other intangibles that make a person what he is — is one of the things we are constantly judged by (by potential lovers and everyone else). Everyone has an opinion about another person's looks. Without hearing her voice, discovering the other aspects of her personality, knowing what kind of work she does, or whether or not she has a pleasant disposition, many men — myself included — know instantly that we would desire sex with the woman with the fabulous legs in a miniskirt, whom we see on the subway.

For some of us, what we consider to be "bad looks" would

instantly eliminate that person from contention as a romantic partner, even if that person possessed fabulous qualities in every *other*
area. Sometimes, we meet someone of the same or opposite sex, and
can't figure out why we don't like this person. His or her looks — as
well as facial gestures or mannerisms — may be the thing that is
rubbing us the wrong way, *irrespective* of whether or not we find
him or her physically attractive.

On *The Dating Game*, three men or three women sit behind a
partition. On the other side, someone of the opposite sex — but
same color — is supposed to pick number 1, 2, or 3 based upon
the person's voice, charm, humor, personality, and how he or she
answered the prepared questions. The reason the questioner does
not see her suitors (using the example of when a woman is choosing
among the three men) is because 99.9% of the time, she would have
already made up her mind as to whom she wanted or *didn't* want to
go out with. There would be no need to ask any of the questions, and
no basis for a show.

On one particular occasion, a tall and attractive female questioner selected a short and unattractive gentleman. The fact that she
picked him indicated that he must have had something in the way of
charm, humor, and a nice-sounding voice. After the host, Jim Lang
said: "And now!...for the man of your dreams"...and the gentleman
came out from behind the screen, the young lady made quite a show
of displaying her disapproval and embarrassment — egged on by
the audience. She smiled while shaking her head horizontally back
and forth, with her palms on her forehead. She could not allow the
audience to believe that this was the man she would have chosen had
she seen him first. I really felt for the man. Not only was he probably
embarrassed, but I'm willing to bet that the young lady refused to go
on the date with him. I am not an advocate of camouflaging one's
feelings, but under the circumstances — on national TV — I felt she
could have displayed better manners and class.

IS THERE SUCH A THING
AS A LOUSY PERSONALITY?

Yes. Everyone has seen people with "bad personalities," but these people think *you* have one, too (even if you were voted "Miss Congeniality" in your high school yearbook). But maybe you caught "Miss Bad Personality" on a bad day. Maybe the fact that she's "the real thing," and doesn't fake *sunniness* when she's in a bad mood, indicates a "good" personality trait. Is this not a better character trait than that of Miss Sunshine...who will exclaim with a broad smile, with all teeth showing, to a person at a party who she hasn't seen in years, and who looks miserable, "How are you?! You look wonderful!"?

The point is, yes; there *are* such things as "bad personalities." But so far, no one has defined what that means.[21]

WHAT IS SEX?

Sex is the (usually) mutual stimulation of the sex organs for purposes of orgasm and/or procreation. Orgasm is (usually) a prerequisite for seminal ejaculation, and seminal ejaculation is a prerequisite for the fertilization of an egg — i.e., for birth.[22]

How important is sex? Just ask all the customers of peep shows, X-rated movie theaters, massage parlors, topless and nude bars, swing clubs, prostitutes, and "adult" bookstores. Just ask the movie industry, and the producers of *Charlie's Angels*.

People crave sex, and are willing to go to great lengths — financially and otherwise — to experience orgasm. The craving for sex is the reason men will jeopardize marriages (even if they happen to be happily married and are having good sex at home), careers, and reputations. They will risk embarrassment, humiliation, and even jail time (in cases where they seek sex with minors or prostitutes).

This universal craving does not spare some of the most extraordinarily intelligent, educated, gifted, and powerful men.

Women, although they take longer to be turned on, love sex just as much as men do. But one does not hear about many women frequenting male prostitutes. Men frequent female — and male — prostitutes all the time.

A plethora of marriages break up because of a lack of sex, or the lack of *satisfying* sex. A man in an otherwise happy marriage is asked why he filed for divorce. "She doesn't satisfy me sexually," he explains. Often, one or both partners seek sex outside the marriage. The sex in the marriage *may* be satisfying, but a partner may wish for variety. A man or a woman may or may not love the person they are having an affair with, but may still love the sex. A man or a woman may be passionately in love with their partner, and may even enjoy sex with him or her more than with the person they are having an affair with.

WHAT MAKES US FALL IN LOVE?

Attraction constitutes a "package deal" based upon our own personal values. Mary may be a stunningly beautiful girl, and Lisa may be merely pretty. Jim, however, is more attracted to Lisa. Jim likes virtually every quality — other than looks — about Lisa, more than he does Mary. Her intelligence; interest in travel, literature, art, music, and culture; ambition, delicious sense of humor, and infectious laugh are all characteristics that Mary can in no way approximate.

At the outset, Jim, and almost all other men, would have picked Mary if they had a choice. Yes, pound for pound, Mary *is* more physically attractive than Lisa. But it doesn't take long for Jim to discover how much more Lisa has going for her. All of the qualities that he discovered she has, have long been strong aphrodisiacs for him. His initial impression had Mary ahead, but as to the entire package, there is simply no comparison. Lisa wins hands down. And when Jim sees her, she begins to *look* more and more attractive all the time.

While he fantasizes about having sex with Mary, he can never go further than thinking of having sex with a merely beautiful body. He simply *adores* Lisa, and when he makes love to her, he experiences an explosive, volcanic orgasm. She has become far more *physically* attractive than Mary, because when Jim looks at her, her physical presence is the embodiment of all the qualities that make her what she is.

WHAT IS A PROSTITUTE? [23]

A prostitute is a person who is in the business of providing sexual acts for money. I will not go into all the situations in which the term might be *technically* appropriate (sleeping with someone for a promotion, marrying solely because that person is rich, etc.). I will speak only in terms of a person who is paid a specified amount of money for sex or sex acts.

DO PROSTITUTES SERVE A PURPOSE?

Just ask the multitude of men who frequent them every day. The question, "Do they serve a *good* purpose?" might more properly be asked. The answer depends on the context and the situation. Assuming that the customer does not contract AIDS or another STD, and nobody gets hurt, then it can serve an arguably useful purpose.

Frequenting prostitutes *can* become an addiction, just like gambling, and only someone of substantial means can frequent them regularly without placing undue financial stress on himself and/ or his family. An exception would be the ugly, over-the-hill street-walkers who are so desperate that they provide their services for a fraction of the cost of the other girls.

⌘

If you're someone like Saudi Arabian arms-dealer and businessman Adnan Khashoggi, and can indulge your passion without financial hardship, then the relationship is mutually beneficial. Khashoggi gets what he wants, and the girls get what they want... knowing that this is the only way they would be able to be rewarded so generously. An astute businessman, Khashoggi also recognizes the value that the prostitutes represent as part of the cost of doing business.

The night before the Super Bowl, it has happened that one of the teams will have prostitutes knock on the doors of players on the opposing team. The cost of the hookers is worth the price of tiring out the players before the day of this all-important game. The ones who pay for the prostitutes know that even though their opponents realize the enormity of the importance of the game, and that they must get their rest, many will not be able to resist the charms of a stunningly beautiful woman.

I have often imagined myself as the quarterback in this dilemma: a conflict between professionalism, the desire to do everything in my power to win the Super Bowl (for my own personal glory and that of the team), achieve notoriety, acclaim, and fame...and pure, undiluted, animal lust. What decision would I make? I'd give in to the latter, but only with the stipulation that it be a "quickie" and that I could get her number...so that we could celebrate *after* my team won the Super Bowl.

Prostitutes serve as an emotionally unattached third party who can offer a man that which his wife cannot or will not provide. They serve as a nonjudgmental sounding board who can provide an aging, unattractive, and out of shape man the illusion that he can be desirable to an attractive young woman. A dishwasher in a diner can suddenly transform himself into a doctor, lawyer, real estate tycoon, CEO, or movie producer in the course of an hour, without having to worry about covering his tracks. They can provide an unhappy, lonely, and unloved man the illusion that he is an important person, even if he thinks otherwise.

But even if it is *not* being used as a temporary fix to alleviate a miserable and unrewarding existence and to fake self-esteem, seeing a prostitute simply for an hour of "no strings attached" fun can serve a purpose…as long as the man understands that her *only* motivation for wanting to see him is money.[24] She also wants to do the least amount of "work," in the shortest amount of time, for the most amount of money. Most of the time, she won't even *fake* pleasure. The man is left with an indefinable sense of bewilderment and frustration over his lack of satisfaction, not to mention the guilt of blowing the money he spent.

He thinks of his friend at work who has a gorgeous wife, available to him both emotionally and otherwise. The fact that he has just had sex *by the meter* with someone who pretends to be friendly — but really hates him — leaves him with a terrible sense of guilt. He now has to go home and pretend to his wife and children that this encounter never happened.

Prostitutes are women who, more often than not, could not make as much money in another endeavor. Sometimes circumstances (such as running away from home to a new city, and/or having no family to turn to) make prostitution a temptation. They are looking for a quick solution to their financial predicament. Others turn to prostitution to support a drug habit. To the majority of intelligent prostitutes, this might not have been the only solution, but may seem like it at the time.

What about prostitutes who claim they love their work? Perhaps it is possible. In some respects, it can be "interesting," as they are meeting new men all the time, hearing new stories (as well as the same ones), and encountering new personalities. They're kind of like horizontal psychiatrists. It's less boring — and pays more — than being a file clerk. But if a career as a fashion model, an actress (the more *traditional* kind), or an executive were offered for similar pay, almost no woman would choose to be a prostitute instead.

WHO SHOULD SEE A PROSTITUTE?

Seeing a prostitute might be a good idea for any man who feels he might die without ever having experienced sex.[25] Assuming the john finds the prostitute physically beautiful, sex *can* be pleasurable, even if divorced from emotional involvement. For a man who craves it, it is not something that should never be experienced at least once during the course of his lifetime. Orgasm, by itself, is one of the miracles of pleasure that nature provides us. When mutual love and admiration are involved, it is one of the ultimate experiences on Earth.

Another man who might do well to visit a prostitute is someone who is married to a 400-pound woman with acne, body odor, rotten teeth, anal warts, and a mustache. Her husband was able to force himself to have sex with her in order to have kids, but after fifteen years, it has become impossible for him to get it up. She's a beautiful and brilliant person, has a great sense of humor, is a good and loving mother, and he *does* care for her. There's just one thing missing, but a very important thing. He knows from the magazines, TV, girls he sees on the beach, and in the office, that there are physically beautiful women he could be attracted to. So he looks elsewhere to satisfy the craving that cannot be satisfied in his marriage.

THE SOLICITATION OF PROSTITUTES

To prosecute a man for attempting to pick up a prostitute, especially a female police officer posing as one, is a gross and deplorable waste of a taxpayer's money. First of all, when a sting operation is involved, most of the time the man does not have the intention of picking up a hooker at that time. It is often a spur of the moment thing. The decoy may be scantily clad and provocatively standing in the street. Because she happens to be very attractive, the man approaches her. Should a man be prosecuted for his sexual desires, especially when he is teased and tricked into propositioning a woman he believes to be a hooker?

Couldn't law enforcement's time be better served trying to arrest violent criminals? A sting operation to catch johns usually involves a *team*: a woman police officer to entrap the man, and a male officer or officers to emerge from their hiding place to swoop down, handcuff and arrest him. This is carried out as soon as the female officer gives them the signal (the man uttering the magic words about financial compensation).

Often, the man is a first-time "offender." Sometimes, he planned to pick up a woman, sometimes he does it on a whim, and sometimes he is entrapped (as described above). The incident often causes severe embarrassment, in addition to jeopardizing families and careers. Those who advocate the publishing of johns' names in the newspaper, or reciting their names on the "john hour" on the news are contemptible. Are these moralizers blaming a heterosexual male for having a normal sex drive? They might as well blame him for having a penis.

I anticipate the counterarguments relating to STDs and AIDS. Sexually transmitted disease has been around for a long time; AIDS came into existence much later. Both can be contracted by irresponsible sexual behavior not related to prostitution (as when a man picks up a woman in a bar, and ends up sleeping with her). Often, STDs are contracted even when both parties are exercising proper precautions. In places such as Amsterdam (where prostitution is legal), it is treated as a profession, and the women are periodically examined by a doctor.

Another objection is that it will bring more drugs and crime into communities. But the primary reason that people object to it is because they want to ram their own concept of morality down other people's throats…often to suppress their *own* latent cravings and feelings of inadequacy. One needs to look no further than the Catholic Church to witness the rampant sexual abuse of children, cover-ups, and hypocrisy.

Should a man who masturbates in a darkened movie theater to a pornographic movie or to a live woman through a hole in the wall at a "peep show" be prosecuted? Paul Reubens (aka Pee-wee Herman), was arrested for public masturbation in a Sarasota, Florida adult theater on July 26, 1991. I could understand arresting a man for masturbating in a public theater where minors are present. But to arrest a man for masturbating in an X-rated theater, where the specific *intention* of the films is to arouse lust, is a grave injustice. It is analogous to the entrapment endemic to the prostitution sting operations described above. It should also be noted that policemen and judges frequent hookers, and masturbate in movie theaters and to peep shows, too. Sometimes the judges who sentence the johns (like the policemen and judges who catch and fine people for speeding, but speed in their own private lives), are caught in embarrassing and hypocritical situations...and incur the wrath of people like Jim Bakker and Jimmy Swaggart.

Jealousy is very often the genesis of moralization. Ugly men and women have been known to hate attractive men and women *because* they are attractive. If they can find a flaw, such as a supposed breach of morality, it makes them feel better about themselves...and subsequently takes away some of the pain of not looking as good, or being as successful. They can consider themselves to be *morally* superior, or more intelligent. But if they loved *themselves*, and felt secure in their own self-worth, they wouldn't need to look for a flaw in another person.

A case in point are the women in the street who try to get people to sign petitions stating that it is degrading for women to be seen in porno magazines. Like the issue of whom you should be allowed to sell your house to, the issue is *freedom*. No woman is being forced to pose for these magazines. The magazines that hire her are paying her to pose, and she has the right to accept or decline. If she declines, the men won't see her in the magazines. If she accepts, the sole purpose of the magazine *having* her pose is to entertain men. Whether or not a woman is "demeaning" herself depends on whatever definition she has of the word "demeaning." She should not have to decline just because a demonstrator who has a different definition of this nebulous word (and is trying to take away her freedom) wants her to. Observe that the overwhelming majority of women who demonstrate over issues such as this are unattractive, and could not get the work that they're trying to keep *other* women from getting. Is it coincidental?

The very men who would denounce Donald Trump and Gary Hart for sleeping with Marla Maples and Donna Rice, respectively, are very often the ones that are insanely jealous that they could never have acquired such a great "piece of ass." Similarly, unattractive women called Maples and Rice sluts, bimbos, and tramps, to give themselves an ersatz sense of superiority, because they knew they could never look as good, or land men like Trump or Hart.

On TV, a film critic once referred to Vanna White's lack of "depth." He might as well have complained about a rock not being soft. Vanna White is a beautiful woman who has an admittedly non-intellectual job. She looks fabulous on TV, and spins the wheel nicely. She is the main reason that *Wheel of Fortune* is one of the most successful shows in television history. She serves the purpose of allowing men all over the world to masturbate without cheating on their wives. She also causes people to ponder one of the most pressing questions of our time: "What will Vanna wear tonight?" She may or may not have the intellect of a rocket scientist; I have no information regarding her IQ. But she sure does have a great SAQ (sex appeal quotient).

WHAT IS MARRIAGE?

Marriage is an accepted ritual of society — which often conforms to specific religious credos — that bind a man and a woman[26] together in what is supposed to be a monogamous relationship "until death do they part." The wife usually adopts the husband's last name, children are usually wished for, and a lifetime commitment is mutually promised when they take their vows. As a corollary, Uncle Sam can usually exploit this contractual arrangement to siphon away tax money that the IRS couldn't have gotten its hands on before the contract was signed.

Is there anything wrong with marriage? No…as long as the man and woman are absolutely convinced, at the time, that their mate is the right person for them. Both should ideally be deeply in love with, and have the highest admiration for, each other. Whether or not they are to be monogamous is to be decided upon by *them*.[27] No one has a right to prescribe what is "right" for them in this highly personal matter. Hopefully, no one gets hurt, but the couple should be free to enjoy the rewards, or suffer the consequences, of their choices.

WHOM SHOULD A PERSON MARRY?

A person should marry whomever they want and can acquire. It is my personal opinion that when one views the person he desires for a mate, he should see fireworks, get goose bumps all over, and be filled with warmth, passion, and love from head to toe. If you have to ask yourself if you're in love with this person, you're not (at least at this time). As was mentioned earlier, "You know it when you see it." Ideally, your mate will represent the "package deal" (also mentioned earlier) of qualities, values, and interests — in all the right proportions — that are important to you in another person. Needless to say, having these feelings reciprocated is ideal. You do not necessarily have to possess all of the same qualities, values, and interests that your mate does, but you *can*, nevertheless, appreciate them.

Is it okay to marry a person for purposes of "status," "social climbing," money, security, convenience, and children…even when love is not involved? Yes. As long as both parties are aware of the motivation at the outset, and are content to marry under these circumstances. If money and social climbing take precedence in their hierarchy of values, then it is not my or anyone else's business to tell them what their "proper" criteria should be.[28]

IS ADULTERY WRONG?

Adultery, in and of itself, is not right or wrong. It's like asking if a waterfall is good or bad. If someone falls in and drowns, then it is *bad*; admired for its natural beauty, it is *good*. If the man and woman support each other's wishes and decisions, then an affair may be engaged in. An affair doesn't always have to be a negative thing. When it receives mutual support in so-called "open marriages," affairs can sometimes revive or save marriages. The important thing is that one does not engage in dishonesty or deceit. Even if the affair is enjoyed, if it is carried out clandestinely, it will carry with it the extra baggage of guilt. The guilt will be the result not only of doing something wrong (cheating), but of lying to cover one's tracks.

If someone is deeply in love with their spouse, why would they want to cheat? There are many answers to this question. Time after time, we hear a man or woman say, "What did I do wrong? I thought I was the perfect husband (wife). How could he (she) do this to me?" The questions come with the assumption that *they* went wrong in some way, that *they* were insufficient. Why else would their partner cheat?

The thing to remember is that most of the time, it is *not* your fault. The man and woman are making their decision based upon their own needs. It may have nothing to do with the partner being a *bad* or unfulfilling spouse.

A seventy-year-old man is deeply in love with his wife. He attends a business convention in another city, and is propositioned by a beautiful twenty-five-year-old woman. The fact that he enjoys the sex does not necessarily mean that his wife is deficient in any way.[29] Perhaps he feels that he has "won" his wife years ago. Maybe he feels that his wife is making love with him not because she is sexually attracted to him, but because this is one of the chores that married couples must perform. The young woman's attraction to him assures him that he can be considered attractive to other women besides his wife. This experience can renew the enjoyment of his sex life with his wife.

Perhaps the man's wife is more beautiful than the twenty-five-year-old, but his encounter was merely "recreational." No matter how much in love he is with his wife, and how much he enjoys sex with her, he does not want to go through life never knowing what it feels like to have sex with another woman.

In conclusion, an affair may be right or wrong for the couple. But *they* should have the right to decide that for themselves — assuming that lying and deceit are not involved — before, during, or after the affair. It is *not* the realm of "religious" people to dictate what individuals should or should not be doing in their private lives, unless their actions interfere with the rights of others.[30]

IS PREMARITAL SEX WRONG?

There is no right or wrong answer to this question. The question might properly be phrased, "Is premarital sex wrong for *you*?" If one's religious beliefs are not in conflict, if the parties do not contract STDs, and if the woman does not become pregnant (assuming she doesn't *want* to) then it's perfectly okay. Perhaps the couple doesn't *want* to get married (which is their privilege).

What does someone do if attracting a compatible member of the opposite sex seems like a hopeless venture? The answer lies within *you*. Is it because you don't love and like yourself, and place others above you in looks, importance, and esteem? Some things simply cannot be changed, but the beauty is that a lot of things — much more than we realize — *can*.

Jack was obese, but he decided, once and for all, that he was going to look like the person that he *could* look like. He embarked on a stringent diet and exercise program. The more weight he lost, the better he looked. And the more his newly adopted diet and exercise program became a habit and a way of life, the less inclined he was to go for that cake and ice cream. He knew how much work it took to get to where he eventually did. What was more important, he would ask himself — to give in to the momentary satisfaction that the cake and ice cream offered (with all the associated guilt), or to continue doing the things he had been doing that got him to the stage he finally reached?

After a year and a half, Jack was absolutely gorgeous. He was actually *always* good-looking, but one couldn't always tell, because of all the fat he was hiding behind. Now Jack dates regularly, and women are enormously attracted to him. But Jack had to make *himself* feel good about Jack, first.

∞

In conclusion, make yourself the best you can be, according to what is important to *you*. If you enjoy being fat, by all means, *stay* fat. (There are many men and women who *prefer* their mate to be fat.) If you hate Spanish, but always wanted to learn French, go to The French Institute, hire a tutor, major in it in college, take a locally available class, or go to France to immerse yourself in the culture and language.

If you hate your nose, get a nose job if you can afford it. If you're a man who is bald, and it conflicts with your ideal image of yourself, get hair transplants. If you're a redhead, and always wanted to be a blonde, dye your hair. Wear a particular cologne or perfume if you feel it is an extension of your personality.

The important thing is that you should be sure the decisions are based on "*self*-direction," not "*other*-direction." Things that cannot be changed (such as height)[31] should be accepted. To spend your life wishing that reality was not reality is an exercise in futility. It is not *better* or *worse* for a man to be six feet tall than to be five foot six. They are merely different heights. If five foot nine is about the average height for men, then both heights listed above are the same distance away from the average. It's what you do with what you have that's important.

Never place anyone above yourself in importance. The wealthy can lose fortunes, and the poor can gain them. People have overcome huge and seemingly insurmountable obstacles. Sometimes, people have recovered from an illness and have walked again, even after doctors told them they never would. People have accomplished and achieved things after other people — including "experts" — told them they couldn't. Contrary to the popular saying, you *cannot* be whatever you want to be, and you cannot always do whatever you want to do. Sometimes, a person has all the ability in the world, but is unjustly barred from a certain profession or avocation. But you *can* constantly improve in the areas that are important to you. And when there is life, there is almost always hope.

CHAPTER 17

The Things We Say

There are many sayings and expressions that are repeated so often that they have become part of the American fabric. Even the ungrammatical sentence "I could care less," has become so common that almost no one knows that "I *couldn't* care less" is proper.

I am frequently told, "I'm going to be very honest with you." This demeaning declaration is uttered so frequently that the ones whom it is directed at don't even realize how demeaning it *is*. If someone says this to you, does this mean they are normally dishonest, but as a special favor, they will be honest with *you*? If they are dishonest with everyone else, why are they giving you this special privilege? And if they are *implying* that they're dishonest with everyone else, why should we think they will be honest with *us*?

"You can be anything you want to be" is a phrase often uttered by parents or teachers as a "pep talk" to youngsters. You *cannot* be anything you want to be. It would be neat to win The New York City Marathon, or to become a basketball player in the NBA. But even if I devoted the rest of my life to the pursuit, did not have to work for a living, and ate, slept, and lived running or basketball, either goal would be beyond the realm of possibility for me. This is not being negative; it is being *realistic*. Eventually, someone will run a sub-two-hour marathon, but no one will ever run a one-hour marathon or a two-minute mile. No matter how much someone trains, and no matter how many advances there might be in training methods, it is physiologically impossible. However, if I were an overweight, unathletic, and middle-aged guy who dreamed of running and *finishing* The New York City Marathon, this would be an incredible personal achievement which would be entirely doable if I devoted the necessary months of training. The phrase might be more accurately worded: "You can be anything you want to be *within reason*," or "You can achieve almost anything that your mind can conceive, if you have a clear goal, and put into place a specific plan of action to achieve it." This also assumes that you *implement* the plan, as nothing will happen without *action*.

There have been many examples of people who achieved incredible things, even when people and "experts" told them that the things they wanted to achieve were unrealistic or impossible.[32] People have been crippled in car accidents, and told by doctors that they would never walk again. Through sheer force of will, and hard work, they did. Amputees have climbed Mt. Everest; children who had grown up in poverty have become multi-millionaires; a blind pianist won The Van Cliburn Piano Competition; a man with no arms became a wrestling champion; Thomas Quasthoff, a 4'3" Thalidomide baby with flippers for arms, became one of the top singers in the world. There are many more examples of what can be accomplished by the power of the human spirit. A love for what they did, the perseverance to go after what they wanted to accomplish, and the fortitude never to quit helped these people achieve their goals. Their *minds*, and what they convinced themselves they could do, played just as much of a role in their success as their physical achievement of the goal.

"Beauty is in the eye of the beholder" is another one of those sayings that is frequently uttered. Because, in certain instances, there *is* truth to the saying, it is repeated to the point of cliché, and accepted as gospel. But the phrase is used primarily as an evaluation of physical attractiveness. If two women who are models or cover girls are evaluated, then the saying may be apt. One person might have a preference for redheads or brunettes; another might like blondes. But everyone has seen people who are considered to be grossly unattractive. Someone who is morbidly obese and/or someone who would be considered conspicuously homely to anyone are examples.

Regardless of what their other qualities might be, in comparison to a Christie Brinkley or an Elizabeth Taylor in her prime, the physical difference is so obvious that a declaration as to the respective attractiveness of these two women, compared to a morbidly obese and/or homely person, is no longer in the realm of opinion. It is a cold, hard fact. There are people who are beautiful *people* and people of monumental achievement, and when we look at them, they *become* more beautiful and handsome, because their looks are the embodiment of their achievements, and who they are as a person. Their looks represent all the wonderful things that make them what they are.

"Everyone is special," "Everyone is a unique individual," "There is genius in all of us," "Everyone has their own unique talents and gifts." These are additional examples of variations of the clichés we hear so often from motivational speakers. They speak to or write books for large audiences whom they don't even know. It sounds so good, is so "inspirational," and is uttered so often that they probably even *believe* this bullshit. But if the above statements are intrinsic characteristics of *all* humans, then how can every person be considered special, just because he is a person? I like to think that the special and constructive accomplishments that people make in the realm of music, art, literature, science, engineering, mathematics, physics, humanitarian work, teaching, sports, inventions, exploration, etc. and being a good human being who lives by the golden rule are what make certain people special. To argue that everyone is special just because they are human is like arguing that God cannot do everything, because He couldn't make a rock so heavy that even *He* couldn't lift it.[33]

Hitler, Stalin, Sadaam Hussein, Pol Pot, Nicolae Caucescu, Muammar Gaddafi, Yasser Arafat, Idi Amin, Kim Jong-il, Fidel Castro, Charles Manson, Ted Bundy, Jeffrey Dahmer, James Ramseur, Mahmoud "Stinky" Ahmadinejad, as well as a decent man who works as a cab driver, and whose only interests are raiding the refrigerator, watching TV, and going bowling are not *special* just because they have different DNA.

TRUE LIES AND HIDDEN MEANINGS[34]

The following are examples of the lies we tell, and their translations.

In the realm of *dating*, a man meets a woman through a personal ad. A week later, he calls for another date. He is told that she has been *so* busy lately that she really couldn't commit to a date at this time. Translation: Although she might consider the man to be a nice person, she has no intention of *ever* seeing him again. She feels uncomfortable with a simple, "No" or "I don't think we're compatible," so she tries to squirm her way out of it, hoping he'll never call again. But if he does, she'll just be "busy" again. The word "really" is thrown in as a softener, as is the word "lately." For a man not versed in the dialect, he might conclude that the door has been left open. But if he calls again, she will still be "busy" (as just mentioned), even though "lately" implied that the situation was temporary. For a man who is more perspicacious, the hurt is greater, but at least he knows where he stands.

When someone tells you how busy they are, they are telling you that they are busi*er* than you. Translation: They and their time are more important than you and *your* time.[35] They *are* busy, as most people are or should be, but not too busy for a date. Why, then, did they *go* on one? And why is it that when women become "busy," it is usually after the first date? Even medical residents and law students studying for their bar exam date; dating is a vital need, like food and shelter. And if they *are* too busy at a particular time, or an emergency situation has come up, the person can always put another date on the calendar if they really want one. Otherwise, they are not too busy for a date; they're too busy for a date with *you*.

A man calls a woman who has responded to his personal ad. She is not getting the proper vibes, so when he asks if she would like to meet, she says, "I think I'll hold off for *now*." Taken literally, this means that she might call him when *now* becomes *later*. But when later *comes*, it then becomes *now*. I wouldn't consider it a good idea to sit waiting by your phone.

In another situation, a man asks a woman over the phone if she would like to meet. She replies, "Well, I don't think we're really hitting it off over the phone." Except for the *really*, it is quite direct. But then she ends with "…so how about if I call you?" Why would anyone want to call someone that they weren't hitting it off with? They wouldn't, but they need a classic beg-off line.

"If I don't call you, it means I'm very busy." Wow! The woman is not going to call you, because she's too busy for *you*, *and* she considers you *less* busy (i.e. important) than she is… because you have time for her, but she doesn't have time for you.

In dating situations, and in all other aspects of life, I'm often told, "I'll try to call you." This statement makes me wonder what the word *try* means. The next question should be "What will determine whether or not you succeed?" Did the person break their dialing finger? Couldn't a pencil be used? Or does it mean "If I find the time to call you…" implying that if they *don't* (find the time) they're too "busy" (for you), and you are not a priority?

These may seem like overanalyzations, but the way people say certain things to you often sends strong messages. Sometimes the recipient finds himself becoming very hurt and resentful of the person, but doesn't know why. Often, it is because the hidden meaning of something they said lies below the surface, and the answer doesn't hit them until much later.

One time, a pianist who played for services at a church had to be out of town, and she asked me to substitute for her. "Richard, *please* play well," she pleaded with me. "The congregation is very sophisticated, and it wouldn't look good for me if you didn't." Translation: "I have doubts that you will play well, because you're not as good as I am."

I had been lax in attending my martial arts classes, and the instructor was considering terminating the classes, as not many people were showing up. "Don't you want to become a better person?" he asked. The martial arts are supposed to help build character, and help you to become a better person…notwithstanding the fact that there are many people who have *not* studied martial arts who were or are fine people. But his statement translated to: "You are not a fine enough person now, and if you don't attend the classes, you won't develop into one. I am still involved in the martial arts, so I *am*. Therefore, I am a better person than you."

A child is told by his mother that if he had any friends, he wouldn't be so bored, and his life would be richer. Rather than suggesting activities that she feels would help him to find friends by increasing his social contacts, as well as his *experience* in interacting with other people, her statement suggests that he does not have friends because he is *unworthy* of them. And *because* he is unworthy of them, it is no surprise that he doesn't *have* any. Yet he is left feeling guilty, inferior, and socially crippled, because he doesn't. Instead of offering help, her brutality inflicts severe pain. What is more, the brutality is intentional.

A husband tells his obese wife that if he ever thought she would turn into a fat horse, he would never have married her. "Do you think a man would really *want* to have sex with a woman who looks like you?" he asks. "If you didn't eat so much cake and ice cream every day, maybe you wouldn't look like that." This is not motivation for his wife to lose weight. It is a cruel and sadistic verbal assault.

The following alternative would have been infinitely more effective: "Honey, I have been reading a lot lately about the incredible benefits of aerobics and resistance training. What's more, they say that when it is combined with drastically reducing sugar, refined foods, avoiding foods that have been over-processed, eating foods in their most natural state, and making sure we get our adequate servings of fruit and vegetables, that it produces incredible benefits. I would love to join the gym that is near us, and hear there are personal trainers there that are excellent, really know their stuff, and know how to motivate people. The trainers at that gym are also highly knowledgeable about nutrition. How about if we make an appointment on Saturday to get a tour of the facilities, check out the programs and the prices, and join together?"

∞

"I might try to call you." This is the double whammy. Because *might* also means might *not*, the person is already indicating that he will not call you. *Try* indicates that he might call if he's *able* to. *Might* and *try* (whatever that means) further decreases to almost zero the probability that you will be called, and is highly insulting to boot. Why is the person announcing what he might do in the first place, if he is not going to do it? It sounds good at the time, but also leaves the person with wiggle room, in case things "come up."

"I'll get back to you," or "How about if I get back to you?" In the former, the person will usually *not* get back to you. In the latter, the person does not want to address your concerns about his owing you money, for example, and needs a way to get off the phone quickly. If you subsequently call *him* back, he'll be sorry he didn't get back to you, but he was *very busy*. If he is so *busy*, how does he have time to speak now? And if he wasn't busy at this time, why didn't *he* call *you*? Often, the reason is because he was "just going to call you."

"I have five calls on hold." Wow! The person is a super-important and busy multitasker and a mover and shaker of the highest order. He must be, to juggle five calls simultaneously. But my favorite, is "I'm on [or I'm expecting] a *long-distance* call." The person must *really* be important.

Returning to dating situations....A woman indicates that she's not interested in meeting a man, but ends the conversation with "I'll speak to you soon."

"I lost your number" is another reason given for not returning a call.

A woman is speaking to a man over the phone for the first time, or she has had one date with him. The man asks for a date, or asks her out again. "I'm going away for two weeks," she says. "Give me a call *then*." The variant is "I'll call you *then*." She is hoping that he won't call, and that the more time she is "away," the less likely it will be that he'll call when she "returns." But she has caller ID, just in case. When he calls, and leaves a message, his call is not returned. Or if she picks up when he calls, she "actually just met somebody." Did she meet somebody when she was away, or right after she got back? If it is the latter, why did she not go out with you first, since you were first in line? It must be because she liked him more. But maybe he just *got there* first. In that case, since she doesn't believe in dating more than one man at a time, she wants to "see if it's going to work out" with him before dating someone else.

One of the most common lines is "I decided to give it another try with my former boyfriend." How coincidental that women "give it another try" with their exes after their first date with *you*.

In personal ads, "Rubenesque," "full-figured," and "curvy," are all euphemisms for "fat." I once asked a woman that I had not met what she looked like. She said, "Womanly." This was a way of answering the question without saying anything.[36] I should have known she would show up morbidly obese.

For women who believe the cliché that a man should never ask her age (even though this is important information to know when you're in a relationship with someone, or contemplating one), the reply "Don't you know a gentleman never asks a woman her age?" is given. Translation: "I am uncomfortable with a fact about myself. The man may think I am too old, and many people consider a woman my age to be less attractive (desirable)." Another retort is "I'm ageless."

In all walks of life, "How are you?" is almost never to be taken literally. It is simply a form of greeting. I *used* to take the line literally, and was frustrated that when I passed someone in a hall that I hadn't seen in months, and he asked, "How are you?" I only had time to utter "Fine" (even when I wasn't). Most of the people who ask, "How are you?" or "How ya doin'?" don't *care* if you stubbed your toe, or your car got towed (no pun intended).

The word *attractive* is not so much a lie as it is a meaningless word. It is the most common adjective that men and women use to describe themselves in the personals. It should follow that a word rendered meaningless by overuse should not cause the reader to form any opinion as to the looks of the advertiser. They say that beauty is in the eye of the beholder (mentioned earlier). *This* beholder has seen the word applied to people he considered to be downright ugly to drop-dead gorgeous. It is also a convenient neutral word that is used when *beautiful* or *handsome* would be stretching their meanings to their outer limits. I have never and *will* never see an ad where someone describes himself as "homely." But wait a minute…I take that back. *I* have posted such ads…to amuse myself, and for purposes of sociological experimentation. And I was thinking of putting the blurbs from all the bad reviews of this book *on* the book, as well as using them in the ads.

Sometimes "softeners" are used as translations, so as to spare the recipient a brutally honest answer. In a creative writing class, students are reading out loud from things they have written for an assignment. A student reads a phrase he wrote on a particular topic, and the teacher is overflowing in her praise. She finds it highly creative and evocative.

Another student reads a phrase *he* has written. The teacher doesn't like it, but calls it "interesting." The student gets the point.

A musician goes to a concert, doesn't like the performance, but wants to go backstage to meet the artist — so he can say, "I shook hands with so and so." "I loved your performance," he says, not knowing what else would be appropriate.

Two third cousins, who haven't seen each other in ten years, meet at a wedding. "You've got to come over and visit us," says one to the other. "Sure," is the response — knowing the offer will be forgotten five minutes later.

John Kerry's presidential campaign against George W. Bush was full of vitriol. But in Bush's classy victory speech (which he didn't write), he referred to Kerry's "spirited campaign." It is proper protocol to be gracious in victory speeches.

LIES AND THE MEDIA

It can be argued that stating that "our fruit punch contains 10% real fruit juice" is not a lie. It probably *does* contain 10% real fruit juice, even though they don't tell you what the other 90% is. It is *technically* not a lie, even though it is dishonest in that it implies the drink is healthy for you. *No added sugar* is listed on the container of juices that contain 26 grams of sugar.

Suppose a defense attorney who was defending the seller of weight-loss contraptions asks the plaintiff, "Yes or no? Can a fat-burning wrap or sitting in a sauna make a person lose weight?

The plaintiff answers, "Yes, but...."

"Yes or no?!" interrupts the attorney.

The judge then asks the plaintiff, "Have you completed your answer?"

"No, your honor," answers the defendant. "Fat-burning wraps and saunas *can* make a person lose weight. But they will only weigh less on the scale, because of their water loss. As soon as they drink liquids, they will gain the weight right back."

A breakfast cereal is advertised during a kids' cartoon show on TV. It is said to be fortified with ten essential vitamins and minerals. The message: It is good for you. Why something good for you should have to be fortified is not explained. Often, sugar is the first listed ingredient. Are the companies getting kickbacks from dentists?

"Our fees are surprisingly affordable." Did you ever see someone leap in the air with shouts of joy after learning what their plastic surgeon's fee would be? Also, the word *affordable* presupposes the question "Affordable to whom?"

ADS AND LIES

When advertising your services in the paper or online, for those who don't know you or don't know *about* you, *price* is usually the most important factor in determining whether or not they will use your services. I give piano lessons, and always run ads. Whether or not people indicate shock at the amount of my fee, a whole host of beg-off lines will ensue: "I'll get back to you" and "I'll call you back for an appointment" are two examples. One of the most common responses I receive when I am speaking to a woman about lessons for her kids is "Let me talk to my husband, and I'll get back to you." Translation: "Your fee is too high. If my husband thinks so too, we would not be interested. And if we're not interested, there would be no reason to call." Not one person who has uttered this phrase has *ever* "gotten back to me."

When potential buyers call a real estate office regarding a house they saw advertised, they are calling to eliminate it. But a good agent will want to show them more homes. Buyers usually do not buy the first thing they see, even if they love it. They usually don't buy the house they called about, either. In addition, they want to know that they first compared a house - even if they loved it - to other homes that were for sale. If they are told too much, there is no reason for them to come in to see the house, so it behooves the agent to get them in the office; he can then show them others. Even if the people are calling because of a For Sale sign, they are often merely curious as to what their neighbors are selling their homes for.

Whatever the case may be, the agent should get a phone number. Even if a particular buyer is not in the market for a home *now*, they may be in the future (or have friends they can refer the agent to who are). If the agent lets the caller hang up without getting a number (assuming the number does not register on his Caller ID), he loses a potential business lead. "I'm calling from a phone booth," or "I'm calling for a friend," are common lines. One agent asked why the friend didn't call *himself*, and was told that he was in the hospital.

Another line is "if I get interested, I'll call you back." An analysis: I'm interested in taking piano lessons, but the price is too high...so I'm not interested. But if a transformation takes place, causing me to suddenly "get interested," I'm sure to call you back. If this were not the reason, the other translation would have been "I'm not interested in piano lessons, but I'm calling anyway, because I *might* get interested." An additional *softener* has been added, too. I wouldn't wait by the phone for this guy, either.

BUSINESS-WORLD LINGO

If you're calling to speak to the decision-maker or head honcho of a company, chances are he'll be in a "meeting," even if that "meeting" happens to be with his secretary, who's giving him a blow job in the bathroom in his office. Translation: "He doesn't want to speak to you."

"He's unavailable." He may or may not be in the office today, but he doesn't want to speak to you. Often, the receptionist will say, "Hold on," in order to first "find out" if her boss is available or not.

What I hate the most when I call a company requesting to speak to someone is a "fill in the blanks" receptionist; I've named them "froms." "Name?" she'll ask.

"Richard Devens," I answer.

"From?"

When I explain that I'm not *from* anywhere (as I don't work for a company), the next question is either "What is this in reference to?" "May I ask what this is in reference to?" (she just did), or "Will he know what this is in reference to?" Each question is to screen you, and to determine whether or not what you want to say to him is worthy of his time. If it's not, then he'll be "unavailable," or in a "meeting."

Sometimes, I have the urge to answer, "That's right," when she says, "From?"

"Say what?"

"Richard Fromm."

THE MIMIC

Did you ever want to badmouth someone? You feel they did you wrong, and you're telling someone else about it. Naturally, you are going to try to slant the whole scenario in your favor, so that the sympathetic listener agrees with you that you were right, and that the other person did you wrong. One way to do this is to mimic what the other person said. And here is where the written word cannot do justice to the real thing…namely all the dialects and caricatures I've heard. To make a visual comparison, it's analogous to the masterful caricatures that Al Hirschfeld created for *The New York Times*. He would take a famous figure, exaggerate a prominent feature, and create a depiction that can be described only as genius.

THE COWARDLY ANTECEDENT

Once upon a time, I was a music major at Brooklyn College. I was sitting in a class, and realized that I didn't know the meaning of a particular term being used. There is a saying that there is no such thing as a stupid question. I happen to tell all my piano students that, as I never want them to go home not understanding something. I also realize that sometimes, it takes longer for something to "stick" with one person than with another. That's okay. Everyone is different, and everyone learns at a different pace. To take myself as an example…I am *not* a quick study. Many pianists can learn and memorize a piece much faster than I can. I wish this weren't the case, but I have accepted my limitation in this particular facet of learning.

That being said, I feel that I have the ability to play most pieces at a high level once I learn them. They also pretty much stick in my fingers and memory, as long as I play them from time to time. If I *haven't* played something in a long while, I can usually get it back pretty quickly (certainly much faster than if I had never learned the piece). If I were on stage performing, it would not matter to the audience how long it took me to learn the piece. The only thing they would be interested in — and cognizant of — was their perception as to the quality of my performance.

Now, let us suppose that another pianist played the same piece I did in the same concert. It took him two weeks to learn the piece, but it took me six months. My performance was more polished, so the audience — without knowing that the other pianist had a greater "talent" for learning and memorizing a piece — will think *I* am the better pianist. This is because the only criterion they would have been made aware of was the *final product*.

But let's get back to the class I was sitting in that day. I realized that if I raised my hand, and asked, "What is a so and so?" I would risk being considered stupid by the professor in front of the class. I thought about equivocating, but decided instead on the more direct or "brave" approach. Sure enough, he responded, "Richard! Haven't I already explained what that was only about a hundred times?!"

In retrospect, I *should* have said, "I know you've already explained what that was, but for some reason, I forgot. Would you please tell me once more?" And while I was saying this, it would behoove me to get my pen out, ready to write down the answer. If I forgot again, at least I wouldn't have to ask him anymore. The professor might have still considered me to be stupid, but there would have been less of a chance of him saying that I "should have known." If he had still said it, it would have been with much less venom, as I had already beaten him to it.

In all aspects of life, people "soften the blow" of what they want to say.

"Can I be brutally honest with you?" A person has something to say to someone that is potentially very hurtful and/or offensive. Rather than just blurt it out, his question acknowledges that the other person might be hurt.

There are hundreds of examples of where this antecedent question is put. A person says to a friend "Can I be brutally honest with you? (The recipient almost always says "Yes," because even though they are apprehensive about what is to follow, they are curious). "Every time you drink too much at a party, you make a real ass of yourself."

Ouch. The person is hurt, but not as much as if the antecedent weren't there. The statement implies that the friend is an ass only when he drinks.

A man wants a divorce, but the prospect of telling his wife is terrifying. George knows that sooner or later, he is going to have to break the news to Beth, but for a few weeks, he can't get himself to take the plunge. The explosion that he envisions, along with the major emotional and financial upheaval that will go along with it, keep him procrastinating. He thinks about just blurting out "Beth, I don't love you anymore. I want a divorce." At least everything would now be out in the open, and the situation can then play itself out. After all, isn't it always better to just jump into a swimming pool than to gently put one toe in after another? The former method instantly acclimatizes someone to the water. The same could be said about pulling a Band-Aid off quickly.

But George can't get himself to do it. He's decided to take the winding road, rather than the expressway; he'll do this even though he feels like a coward, and it prolongs the agony.

"Honey, we've been married almost fifteen years now. I want you to know that it has been a great honor to know such a special woman. We've enjoyed great times together, have traveled all over the world, produced two great kids, and been through a lot. But for the last couple of months, I've kind of been thinking that sometimes it's better to move on, and see what else is out there, while still cherishing the memories. What I'm trying to say, is that it has nothing to do with you. You didn't do anything wrong. It's just that I feel, perhaps, that it would be best at this stage to go our separate ways."

George still gets hit with the explosion and tears. The former method would have been admittedly too abrupt and abrasive. He's doing all he can to lessen the impact (which is commendable), even though he feels slightly cowardly.

THE "BUT MASTER"

Which side of the "but" we place a phrase or sentence on will color and manipulate the recipient's perception as to which half is of greater significance. It doesn't have to be two sentences, however. It can be two people's recounting an incident or set of circumstances. Whatever comes after the "but" acts as a rationalization or denunciation of the same actions (depending on the point of view of whoever is arguing the rectitude of their case).

Here is a scene in a courtroom. A prosecuting attorney is giving his closing arguments.

"Yes," he says. "Some people *have* been brought up under trying circumstances. We can never minimize the impact that having an alcoholic parent has on a child. And I'm not going to try to pretend that living with Mr. X was a bed of roses. But one of the tenets of the American system of justice is that we don't take the law into our own hands. If we killed everyone who we thought was doing something wrong, then what would we need courts for? We would be living in a society of anarchy. Ladies and gentlemen of the jury….Please review the evidence and facts of this case, and find the defendant guilty as charged."

The attorney acknowledges what the jury members would undoubtedly be thinking; his concession caters to their sense of right and wrong by legitimatizing their emotional reaction to physical abuse. In so doing, he portrays himself as "human." Now, he can argue his case after the "but," and be even more persuasive.

Earlier, when Gina was on the witness stand, she faced the jury and said, "You know…a lot of you are going to be swayed by the prosecutor. He's going to say I killed my father, and he'll be right. I *did* kill my father. And because of that fact, you will be instructed to find me guilty. Then I'll be sent to prison. But even though I'll be put away, it won't be to 'rehabilitate' me; it will be to punish me… but not for something I did wrong. I will be punished for what the *law* says I did wrong." She then goes on to paint a picture of the conditions she was living under.

"Ever since I was a little girl, I was beaten and sexually molested by my father. I would also see him touch my little sister in bad places. For years, I never told my mother, because I was too ashamed. But when I did, she was too afraid to help me. My father had threatened that if she ever said a word to anyone, he would kill her. Eventually, he started beating her regularly, and I would cry helplessly in my room, as I didn't know what to do.

"One day, he was choking her, and I was afraid he would kill her. I ran into the room, and started beating his back with my fists.

'Please don't hurt Mommy,' I said. He picked me up, threw me against the wall, and said, 'Mind your own business, you little bitch.' Luckily, he passed out after that, as I really felt he was going to choke Mommy to death.

"When he got into an argument with my mom the next night, he started slapping her around. I guess I just snapped. I ran downstairs to the kitchen, grabbed the butcher knife, and plunged it into his back. Yes, I know I killed him. But in order to understand someone's motivation, you have to be able to walk in his shoes, live in his skin, feel what he's feeling, and understand his context.

"Maybe I *should* have gone to the police, but even if we got an order of protection against him, what would stop him from killing us in revenge? Put yourself in *my* place. What would *you* have done?"

So here we have it. Two people are talking about the same incident and circumstances. But each puts the same occurrences in a different light. The attorney wants to win his case; he puts the "but" *before* the reason why he asserts Gina should be found guilty. Gina paints a more complete and descriptive picture of the set of circumstances she was living under. She admits to what she has done, and justifies it with many "buts."

"I hired Roy Cohn," a client once told a *60 Minutes* interviewer, "because he's a tough son of a bitch." When you call or refer to a person as a "son of a bitch," it is a pejorative description. But used in the above context, the person was paying the late attorney a compliment. Part of what made Cohn so successful was that he *was* a son of a bitch. Very often, the attorneys who are the most successful are the ones who can set aside their feelings. They are not paid to be "nice,"

and they are not paid to be ethical. They are paid to win, and to win at all costs.

THE DISCLAIMER

The *disclaimer* is a cousin of the *"but master."* His proclamations need the word "but" in the middle to contradict his antecedents.

"I'm not prejudiced," an agent in a real estate office once told me, "but those customers acted like typical Indians."

"Not to belabor the point," someone will say. Then he'll proceed to belabor it after the "but."

"Not to read too much into it," "Not to dwell on the things which were already said…." The list is endless. The person knows he will be accused of being redundant or repetitive, so he precedes his declaration with a disclaimer in the antecedent. If he *is* accused of being redundant, then he beat his accuser to it, and deflected whatever criticism he might have received. It is similar to what I said I *should* have done when I asked the music professor a question.

ARE ALL LIES BAD?

Lying is not *always* bad. In a case where no harm is done to another person, but you can get hurt if you *don't* lie, then I highly recommend it. Dr. Wayne Dyer uses the example, in one of his books, about a highly qualified woman who looked much younger than her age, but was repeatedly being turned down for jobs *because* of her age. Her would-be employers were operating under the assumption (lie) that a person of her age would not be as qualified as someone younger.

When I was a real estate agent, I was a *listing* specialist; I would get *exclusive listings* on homes, which others would sell. Some would say that a listing agent is even *more* important than a selling agent (although occasionally, they are one and the same), because you have to have a listing first, before it can be sold.

If I were out with a customer, and asked how many homes I sold that year, I would always feel morally obliged to take the question literally and to mention only homes that I had actually sold myself (which were very few). I didn't mention the listings of mine that had been sold (which were many). If I had answered, "Many," I probably would not have been "lying," because a listing was *part* of making a sale. A customer might not even have known what a listing is, much less the distinction. But at the time, I felt a need to be *technically* honest, even though it caused me to lose credibility. Often, the questions "How many homes have you sold?" and "How long have you been in the business?" are put-down questions. Who would want to work with an agent who sold only one house, or just started working yesterday?

Looking back many years later, the word that comes to mind when assessing my behavior is not *honesty*, but *stupidity*.

CHAPTER 18

Verbal Aikido

*A*ikido is the *gentle* Japanese art of self-defense. One uses the force of another person against him. Sometimes, we are attacked verbally, and the severity gets lost in translation. Speaking personally, a delayed reaction often occurs, and I am hit with the true meaning of the vitriol a few hours or a day later. Some examples were cited earlier. Often, the meaning is evident right away, however, and we want to defend ourselves.

Sometimes, insults from people we know, or in dating situations, can hurt much more than obscenities from random strangers. People who are driving yell variations of "fucken scumbag," "fucken asshole," and "cocksucker" at one another. The words and expressions don't really mean anything; they are all interchangeable — any one could easily be substituted for another. Nobody could ever specify what the difference between a "fucken asshole" and a "scumbag" is. What is *not* ambiguous is the total contempt, hatred, and rage that one person has for another. Let's not dance around it; when someone gives you the finger, or calls you the epithets above, they despise you, and want you dead. They would celebrate if they were able to find out that you had contracted terminal cancer. If they could press a button and blow you up to smithereens without punishment, they would do so.

But if a woman whom you meet on a date for the first time tells you that she sees no reason to go through with the date, as she doesn't find you attractive at all, that's another story. Although she might not have been specific as to which body parts she didn't like, it wasn't necessary. When we see someone for the first time, we instantly pass judgment as to whether they are attractive or not. But when you *tell* someone they're not "attractive," that hits very hard and deep. Everyone wants to feel that they are attractive and are presenting an attractive appearance to the outside world. Ninety-year-old wrinkled women go to the beauty parlor. Women whom the average person would consider to be grossly unattractive take out pocket mirrors to smooth out a strand of hair and dab on lipstick. They wear contact lenses.

Being honest when honesty will unnecessarily hurt someone is not necessary. To a date, or potential date we may not be physically attracted to (either in person, or from a photo), "You're not my type," or "I don't think you're the right one for me," or "I don't feel the necessary chemistry," will do. The person makes it a "vibes" thing without attacking them personally. But if a person deliberately goes for the jugular, you have every right to fight back.

Ben goes on a date with Janet, a personal trainer, and at the end of the date, asks her if he can see her again. She replies, "I don't think so. Can I be brutally honest with you?" Even though Ben has steeled himself for what is to follow, he says, "Yes." Janet continues, "You don't look *anything* like your photo. I was expecting someone who was really in shape, and there's no way you could describe yourself as being fit. In the future, you really shouldn't misrepresent yourself."

Ouch, that hurt. Ben is feeling really guilty, too. He thinks that maybe he *is* a liar and has been deceptive. He is very much into health and fitness, but because of a recent operation and situations in his life, he has slacked off his workouts the last couple of weeks; he started eating things he normally avoided. He also gained about fifteen pounds. Although he *is* a little flabby, he is only about a month away from getting back into pristine condition again if he really buckles down. But there is no way Ben is going to just slither away without saying anything back.

He notices that, as in her photo on the dating site, Janet in no way, shape or form has a beautiful face. But when it came to women, Ben was always much more of a "body" than a "face" man. He would rather have a girl with a great body and a not so great face, than vice versa. He tells Janet, "You know, I'm sorry you feel that way. I don't like your face at *all*; all of the other women on the site were so much prettier, but I was interested in *you*, because you have one of the most amazing bodies I have ever seen. That really turns me on in a woman. But take care, anyway."

This is masterful. Janet thinks Ben has tried to compliment her, because he has put the *positive* on the other side of the "but." But Ben purposely phrased the sentence that way, so as to slip the negative in (without making it *sound* like he is trying to insult her). By speaking so glowingly about her body, it makes it *seem* as if he wanted to pay her a compliment. So his retort is infinitely more effective and believable than it would have been had he replied, "Well, you don't look so great, either."

That night, Janet goes home and spends a lot of time in front of the mirror. She has always been insecure about her face, and secretly knows she can't hold a candle to a *Vogue* cover girl, no matter how great her body is. She is deeply upset, because Ben's remark hurt her as a woman. Maybe in the future, Janet will be a little more discreet and sensitive in her dealings with men.

"Can I ask you a stupid question?" Once, a woman asked me this highly insulting and sarcastic question, when she thought I had done something stupid. I stupidly replied, "Yes," because I hadn't thought of the perfect comeback at the time: "You just *did*."

It's amazing how a professional comedian can make mincemeat out of the average person in the audience. You can always tell who the pro is. They also have the advantage, in that *they* are holding the microphone. I was really happy to see Don Rickles give it to David Letterman one night. He totally out-humored him, and put him in his place...just like Letterman might have done to a random member of the audience.

Jay Leno has had "fat" sketches on his show, where he plays an obese man slobbering over junk food. One time, he made fun of a man in the audience with a protruding stomach. As Leno patted his belly, the man just sheepishly smiled. How I wish that just once, an average Joe in the audience would out-humor a Letterman or a Leno. The perfect retort would have been, "You know, Jay....With my belly, and your chin, we'd make a perfect team!"

Originally, I was going to include the following in the previous chapter, because equivocating and beating around the bush are examples of "the things people say." But *what* we say, and how we say it are also determinants of how well we've mastered the art of verbal aikido.

Throughout life, people are going to ask you to do things that you don't want to. "I don't want to do it," said in a friendly, but forceful and direct manner, lets the other person know, unambiguously, where you stand. If you answer, "Well, I don't know..." you leave an opening for the person to wedge himself in: "Oh, come on...pleeeeese?!...pretty please?" If you end up doing what the other person wants, you end up hating yourself for it, while resenting the other person, to boot. If the other person ends up resenting or disliking you for making a choice in *your* best interest, ask yourself if that person was *worth* doing a favor for, or committing your time to.

Money is *not* something you should be lending people (especially family and friends) unless you enjoy being a lender, and don't care if you don't get paid back. Relationships have been severed on account of it. Let's say someone is hard up for cash, comes to you, and asks you to lend him money. He promises to pay it back at a specified date. Against your better judgment, you lend the money, because you want to be thought of as a "nice guy" or a "true friend."

Here is the problem, however: Unless the person has undergone a major financial breakthrough, chances are he'll be just as "hard up" when the time comes to pay you back as he is now. What also must be factored in is that life doesn't always cooperate with our plans. How often has the following situation happened? You had an important business appointment about fifty miles away. You figured you'd leave early, and have lunch at one of your favorite restaurants close to where your appointment is. You are already planning what you are going to order, and can even taste the food in your mind's palate. You're worried about what you're going to do if you get there too early, but remember that you were planning to look over a couple of magazines, before throwing them out. You could take care of that there.

You get on the highway, and find yourself daydreaming about the pleasant things you have planned. Because of this, you miss an exit. But no problem; you could just go another way. It's a little longer, but still gets you to the same place. All of a sudden, everything comes to a grinding halt. The highway is now a giant parking lot. For two hours, nothing moves. Emergency vehicles are summoned to remove the truck that jackknifed four miles down the road.

Similarly, the time comes when the person promised to pay you back, or to make a payment. You remind him of it, but he tells you that the transmission on his car just went, and it's going to cost a fortune to have it replaced. You remind him of his promise, but he asks how he's supposed to pay you back now, if he has to get his car fixed? How can he go to work to get money if he has no wheels? Sometimes, there is a death in the family. If you ask for your money back at *this* time you're not only afraid of being insensitive; you feel like a monster. But what if *your* transmission goes at this time, or you suddenly find out that your home needs major repairs? Is this fair to *you*?

Observe that regardless of someone's personal problems or circumstances, airlines, restaurants, stores, telephone and electric companies, and any business expects to get paid when services are rendered. Would the shop where the person is getting his transmission fixed agree to let him pay "in a few weeks" when things "get back together again"? But yet, *they* are not being "insensitive."

If you *give* money to someone whom you want to give it to, that eliminates the uncomfortable position of not getting your money back when you were promised. Life has a way of screwing up plans, and doesn't always go by the script we hope or envision it will.

CHAPTER 19

The Rude Brood

There's no way around it. Just like death and taxes, they're here to stay. Someone will hold a door open for you, and just as you're about to say "Thank you," they'll say "You're welcome." Now you have a dilemma. Should you say "Thank you" now that they have been rude and sarcastic, or should you not say anything and have them feel self-righteous for being sarcastic to a person whom *they* deem rude?

An even ruder person said, "Excuse you," as I was navigating through a crowded room to my destination. Apparently, I had come too close for comfort, and I was the one being rude for not saying "Excuse me." I never try to be rude, and always remember to say "Please" and "Thank you." But no matter how hard I try, I encounter rude people, as well as people who think *I'm* rude.

People talk at the movies and at classical music concerts. Other than in an emergency, what could there possibly be to talk about? Some people think that mouths are meant to stuff their faces and for chattering...even when they're not saying anything. I rarely go to movies. When I do, I want an escape, and I want to concentrate totally on the dialogue and plot. Why must I always be sitting near someone who is offering a companion a running commentary on everything that's going on? When Ali McGraw spread Skippy peanut butter on a slice of bread in *Love Story*, a woman said, "Skippy peanut butter." Was it to let her companion know she could read, or to fill him in on something he might have missed?

An actor will appear on screen. "My, he aged!" someone will say. One time, someone was telling someone exactly what would happen in one of the scenes before the movie came on! I didn't enjoy the movie, because I was distracted by the anger I felt toward someone who would ruin the experience for me. Before I saw *Rocky* for the first time with a group of kids from camp, a kid who had seen the film the previous day announced to all of us that Rocky and Apollo Creed knocked each other down at the same time. Never having seen that in a real boxing match, I would have loved *not* to have known what happened...especially since I considered that to be the climax of the entire movie. Needless to say, that kid was not one of my favorite people.

In two particular movies, the punch line of the whole film is revealed in the last sentence. But a woman sitting in front of me leaned over to tell her husband what it was. In my fantasy, I was screaming, "Why the fuck don't you shut up and let people who aren't as smart as you enjoy the movie and find out for themselves?!"

Sometimes, people don't *mean* to be rude, but certain customs are accepted as proper protocol. It is done so often that it is accepted as normal. In *The Success Principles*, Jack Canfield writes that if you're being helped by someone, and the phone rings, the person who called should wait in line behind you, as you were being helped first. I completely agree, even though it doesn't work like that in the real world.

I was sitting in an administrator's office discussing group health insurance coverage, when his phone rang. It was another employee, calling regarding the same issue. I sat there for about fifteen minutes while he "took care of" her first. She was calling from the comfort of her home; I had come to his office in person. I didn't think of it at the time, but maybe if I called him on my cell phone while I was sitting right there in front of him, he would have put the employee on hold, and taken care of me first.

I never do my banking at a drive-through window. I'm always more comfortable going inside. I can get things out of my pockets more easily, and feel more "organized." But if there happens to be only one teller on duty, and I was there first, the teller will *always* service the drive-through customer first.

Sometimes someone wants your attention in the street. Perhaps he wants directions. He'll say, "Hey, Mack!" "Yeah? What do you want, Bugsy?" would be an appropriate comeback. Bugsy doesn't sound like an overly sophisticated name, so the guy might take offense. I never thought of it at the time, but admit I might not have the nerve to say it. But if you have any self-esteem, and you don't like a name you're being called, I would recommend that you ignore it.

Once, someone called out to me, "Hey asshole." I had pulled ahead of him into a parking garage five minutes earlier. When I ignored it, looked straight ahead and kept walking, he repeated it. Still not getting any response, he said, "You're a fucken scumbag." I had "won" the encounter, because Fucken Scumbag wasn't even sure I had heard him, or that I knew he was talking to me.

Doctors *love* their title. They worked and studied so hard for it, that they now can use it as a status symbol and weapon. They're not trying to be rude, but they can call you by your first name, even though you can't do likewise. I *always* prefer being called by my first name. If Mack doesn't happen to know it, then "sir" would be acceptable.

Did you ever notice that there could be a group of people who all refer to each other by their first names? One of them is a medical doctor, however, and he is referred to only as Dr. Jones. I used to drive for a car service. The dispatcher would tell us to pick up Jim at a particular address, Dave in front of a business, or Sue at an air terminal. But when it was a doctor, it was always Dr. Anderson. One time, when

I was in the real estate business and doing an open house for a family, I addressed the owner as Mr. Smith. This man happened to be a scientist with a PhD, and immediately corrected me: "*Dr.* Smith."

Dr. Wayne Dyer writes in one of his books that he is always on a first-name basis with everyone. He puts it very well, when he says that if he *does* call someone by a title, it is because that person *needs* to have one. The translation: He needs one to maintain a "status symbol," and to use this as ammunition to elevate himself above others in importance. Ironically, I have seen many men and women without "Dr." before their last name who were far more renowned and accomplished in their respective fields than most doctors are in theirs. And they made more money, too.

The caste system in India, as well as what constitutes "royalty" in England, are total bullshit. People are not "better" than others, just because they happen to be born into a certain family. They *earn* their status by their achievements.[37] The late Shana Alexander of *60 Minutes* once put it very well when she said that Queen Elizabeth is a "boring housewife." I don't put much credence in whom she taps on the head with a sword to knight "Sir." And I applaud Beethoven (even though this colossal genius was crude and rude in his dealings with people) for refusing to step out of the way when "nobility" was passing.

In business situations, the overwhelming majority of people do not return phone calls. This rude behavior is just a fact of life. Unless it is a case where they stand to benefit financially, ignoring someone's call has become an accepted (and expected) behavior. I am a pianist; a lot of my work has come from cold calling: Does this restaurant need a pianist? Does this music school need a piano instructor? If I leave a message — either by voice mail or with an employee — and my services are not needed, I will not receive a call back.[38] But if I were to leave a message saying I was interested in having my wedding at the restaurant or catering hall — or taking lessons at the music school — my call would be returned immediately.

In dating situations, if you ask someone out again, and are told, "Call me," your call will almost never be returned if the person is not interested.

Sometimes, I have received the message on my answering service: "Hi, this is Joe. Please call me at___." Wanting to practice what I preach, and not wanting to be "rude," I returned the call. Joe turned out to be a solicitor asking for money. He knew I would not have called back, had I known the nature of his call. Obviously, I am not being rude if I don't return a call such as this.

∞

How do you deal with rude people who don't return calls? I have adopted the "*two call* rule."

This rule states that I will call and/or e-mail a person a total of two times (in any combination). If I don't receive a response, I will permanently eliminate them from my life. I don't have to worry about "Why aren't they calling me back?" "What if they didn't get the message?" "What if I call a third (or fourth) time? Might they call back then?" The decision is already made for me, and just like hanging up on a telemarketer, the situation receives closure immediately.

Why the "*two call* rule?" Even though there is 99% certainty that the person received your message the first time, there have been instances of a malfunction in the answering service. A child may have erased the message before the person received it. A cell phone might not have been charged. An e-mail might have gone to the person's spam. But after a second attempt, the person has received the message with almost 100% certainty. In my younger doormat days, I would call people continuously. If a person didn't call me back on the second attempt, they didn't on the tenth.

Is it rude to hang up on telemarketers? Not if you value your time. I used to allow them to remain on the line, and hold on to me like a leech. A solicitor from my alma mater would enquire how I was, and engage in pleasantries. He'd finally get to the point: a $500 donation to the university. I happened not to have had many fond memories of my alma mater, and had enough trouble trying to make ends meet, myself. I would say, "I'm sorry, but I can't afford to make any donation."

"I completely understand," would be the response. "But would you be able to make a $250 donation?" Even though I had already said I couldn't make *any* donation, the solicitor would just keep asking for a lower amount. I knew this would continue indefinitely, and felt guilty and uncomfortable for being "cheap." I didn't want to be "rude." I ended up being rude to my*self* for not respecting and valuing my time. I have learned to say, "I'm sorry, but I can't make any donations," and immediately hang up. That ends the situation on the spot. You don't have to ask anyone's *permission* to end a conversation, much less an intrusive one.[39]

Restaurants should provide a pleasant dining experience. Sometimes the food might be good, but if the service is poor, you end up not enjoying it. I rarely eat steak, but if I do, I want to eat it while it is still hot. If the waitress forgets to bring a sharp cutting knife, all you have is the butter knife that you used for buttering your bread. But at these times, the waitress has disappeared. Meanwhile, you do not want to eat until you get your sharp knife.

Often, it is so hot outside, that the glass of water I received is insufficient for quenching my thirst. The food has already arrived, but all I can think of is how thirsty I am. If I start eating, I am not enjoying the food, because I am concentrating on finding the waitress, getting her attention, and having my glass refilled. But as in the above example, that is when she has usually disappeared. Often she is serving or taking orders from other diners. But when she walks past, she does not make eye contact, and before I can get her attention, she is already with other customers, or has disappeared to the kitchen.

At times, I've enjoyed the meal, but ended up not enjoying the experience. I've finished eating, the waitress is not to be found, and I can't get my check. Sometimes, I've wanted to order dessert, but ended up getting so angry that I decided not to. All I wanted was to pay my check and get out of there.

When the check finally comes, if you intend to pay by credit card, your exit can be greatly delayed. If the service is decent, I usually double the tax to determine the tip. It takes a few seconds to scan the check to see if there are any items that you were erroneously billed for, and to see what the tax is. The waitress should stay there a few moments, but usually walks away.

If you have cash, and the proper denominations, you can put everything on the table and leave. But if you want to pay by credit card, you need the waitress to return and pick it up. But as in the examples above, she usually disappears. Exasperated, I look at my watch, and start deducting from the tip for each self-specified time period that I am held captive. Often, there is a ball game on the car radio that I'm dying to hear, or things I have to take care of at home. But the waitress is often having *her* meal, is talking with other workers, and is completely oblivious to me.

One time, a waitress dropped off the check and left. Finally, I had to get up, find her, and give her my card. I signed it, got up to leave, and only *then* did she eagerly rush back to my table to find out the amount of her "reward." Unfortunately for her, I drew a dash through the tip column.

Waitresses should be trained to periodically check up on their customers. I do realize that sometimes a waitress is taking an order from another table, and cannot always immediately cater to you. All I'm asking is that they continually scan their clientele to efficiently take care of their needs as fast as possible. In the rare instances when the food has been great, and the service exemplary, I will leave a very generous tip. But I do not feel I should be obligated to leave *any* tip if I have had an exasperating experience.

Once, I left a tip for a rude waiter, and ended up hating myself for it. He might have followed me outside (as has happened), or made a nasty remark. But if he did, why would I *want* to leave a tip for somebody like that?

I believe in tipping. Waiters and waitresses depend on it, because their salaries are so low. But I also believe a tip should be for enjoyable, competent, and friendly service. If you leave a tip for *in*competency or rudeness, then you are condoning it. If you don't leave a tip, you might be cursed, but you will almost never be physically attacked. After all, you know where this person works, and it would not be difficult to find him if you wanted to press charges.

Don't leave a tip for terrible and/or rude service. If you reinforce this behavior, by leaving a tip, you are telling that person it's all right to treat you this way.

CHAPTER 20

The Law Of Averages

It has been said that if someone tries, tries, and tries again, the *law of averages* will ensure that sooner or later, he will be successful. We have all heard the anecdote about Thomas Edison being asked if he was discouraged by all the times he failed at making a light bulb. He is said to have replied, "No. I just learned X amount of ways *not* to invent a light bulb." And eventually, he was successful.

But we've also heard that the definition of insanity is doing the same thing over and over again, and expecting a different result. How do we reconcile the two statements? I think that the statement "Luck is when preparation meets opportunity" should be thrown into the mix.

There is truth in both of these statements. But imagine some-one who hadn't taken a shower for a week, didn't shave, and didn't change his clothes. He wants to meet a beautiful woman, hears of the law of averages, thinks it sounds neat, and is willing to work within its parameters. He goes all over the city, riding the subway, going to museums, strolling down the street, walking through Central Park, etc. because he has been assured that if he gets enough "No's" from women he asks for a date, eventually one will say "Yes." But Charlie is operating under a misguided assumption. The law of averages doesn't always kick in just because a guy is putting up the proper numbers. Charlie's probability of dating a beautiful woman from his escapade is almost zero.

Now, contrast Charlie with Frank. Frank knows that he is going to incur massive rejection. Married women will be insulted; some women might have considered going out with him, but have a boy-friend. Some women, in this day and age, will be very wary of a guy bold enough to walk up to them in the street and ask for a date. He will receive a lot of insults and rude comments. But Frank is totally prepared. He has been working out at the gym religiously. He gets his hair cut and styled, buys a tailor-made suit, makes sure his shoes are shined, and his hygiene is impeccable. No detail is too insignificant. Unlike Charlie, Frank has the numbers on his side. The law of averages says that since Frank is so prepared, and is willing to do whatever it takes (approaching every beautiful woman — not with a man — he sees), he has about a 100% chance of eventually finding a woman who will say "Yes."

CHAPTER 21

The Sound Barrier

I *hate* noise, but I'm not a *misophoniac*. Misophonia is a hatred of sound in which ordinary, everyday sounds — regardless of volume — can drive someone into a rage. Hyperacusis is sensitivity to all sounds, including normal environmental sounds. But according to the definition, I do exhibit *some* of the symptoms associated with misophonia.

To try to be more specific…as a classical musician, my hearing is very important to me, and I have a hatred of sounds that I feel can damage it. That, plus the physical pain I experience, drive me crazy. I *love* certain sounds, such as beautiful music. I don't mind the sound of the crashing waves of the ocean on a beach, or the sounds that seagulls and birds make. Those sounds represent nature to me. I do *not* like deafening thunderclaps, because the decibel level is beyond my tolerance.

I hate certain repetitive sounds. A car siren that maintains the same pitch, and does not turn off for hours, is literal torture. So is a recurring honking horn. A neighbor who has a little garden close to my bedroom window keeps a cell phone outside, which keeps ringing in close proximity to my ear. No one picks it up, so it will ring about five times before stopping. A short time later, the piercing rings will begin again.

Another neighbor has chimes hanging from her terrace. When it is windy, they are very loud. In the nighttime, why should this be considered any different from someone playing a TV, radio, or musical instrument at a loud volume? Indeed, I am often abruptly woken up by what sounds like a loud xylophone being played next to my ear.

The condo development in which I live is horrendously constructed. The creaking and snapping of the floor when my upstairs neighbor walks — in addition to the slamming of the drawers — is excruciating. It is even more so because he walks back and forth into the wee hours of the morning. Sometimes his bedsprings rhythmically vibrate like a locomotive chugging toward its destination. The sound accelerates in tempo and continues to crescendo in tandem with the accompanying moaning. Suddenly, there is a scream of ecstasy, and the locomotive stops.

I abhor motorcycles. Once I stepped outside a restaurant as a motorcycle approached. I couldn't reach my ears in time to soften the deafening roar. Even as it passed, the sound kept getting louder and louder. It was like a hundred machine guns were all firing at the same time, amplified with a microphone. I feared for my hearing, and couldn't stop thinking that if I hadn't stepped outside the restaurant at just that time, I would have been spared the assault.

When there are commercials on TV or the radio, sometimes a speed talker is hired to recite the small print of the disclaimers of the drugs which are advertised. As in music and speech, sound must *breathe*. I must rush to turn off the monotone. Some sounds, at certain venues, are criminal, such as a cell phone going off, or a baby crying during a performance of *Winterreise*.

Planes landing at an airport, and flying at low altitudes, should *not* be flying over residential neighborhoods. Garbage trucks or buses in the middle of the night that screech until they stop; trucks that are stopped, but idling at a constant sound — because the ignition is not turned off — and cars with faulty mufflers are other offenders. A dog that barks, and will not stop, is too much to bear.

Buzz saws are not only deafening, but they emit a grinding sound similar to that of a dentist drilling, but amplified many times over. The firehouse lets off about five sirens, which last a long time. But at least I know that that is their quota for the day.

What about lawn mowers and leaf blowers? If I am the only one who finds the noise unbearable, why do the operators often wear sound-canceling headphones? Does this equipment *have* to be that loud? I fear Tuesdays, because this is the day the landscaping company comes to do the lawns. I always have to time my run to the car when there is a lull in the noise. I know they are employees, and are being paid to do this work. But nevertheless, I instantly hate them. I have named the leaf-blower operators, who carry the motors on their backs, the "suicide bombers."

Vacuum cleaners are on the list, as well. Sometimes, the only time I had to frequent a particular restaurant was at 3:00 p.m. (their off-hour). That was the time they determined was best to vacuum. It was not an enjoyable dining experience. And screaming babies always seem to know which table I'm sitting at. Likewise, the hosts and hostesses always seem to seat me next to the bins where the dirty dishes — to be hauled off to the kitchen — are placed. I have to endure the sound of the plates as they crash into one another.

The weight room at the gym is another place that engenders fear in me. Iron crashing against iron as people rack their weights is painful, and incites my wrath. I keep telling myself I will bring earplugs next time, but for some reason, I never do.

I hate sound for the sake of sound, which is why the 4th of July is one of my least favorite dates. What does the shooting off of firecrackers (explosives) have to do with celebrating a holiday? I can appreciate a fireworks display — if performed in the distance, by professionals, over an ocean or river.

The hallways of grade schools are loud, what with hundreds of kids bunched together. It is a veritable cattle migration. Sometimes, a girl will emit a shrill scream for no particular reason. I consider screaming in my ear to be a physical assault.

Why do restaurants and bars always have to have music playing in the background? Why must someone who hates a particular song or style of music have to endure it, just because the person who put it on likes it? Shouldn't everything be done for the benefit of paying customers? "But what of the customers who like the music?" one might ask. I would reply that if there were *no* music, there would be no chance of someone not liking it. Why is it that 5-star restaurants *never* have music playing?

I have been in restaurants where the music was so loud that I was unable to carry on a conversation. This is the norm at most bars. If it is a pickup joint, and two people meet, how are they to communicate with one another? Sometimes, the music is not even the issue. In some places, tables are placed in close proximity to one another, there is no carpeting or padding, and having a large crowd produces a loud cacophony. This happened at a recent speed dating event I attended, and I found myself literally unable to carry on a conversation. I could not hear the speaker, and was embarrassed that I had to ask her, four times in a row, what she said. I couldn't hear myself, either, so I had to scream. One particular woman had a piercing laugh and voice, and was situated in a spot where the sound rebounded as if amplified by a microphone. When sitting close by to her, and trying to talk with another woman, it not only was painful, but I was worried about my hearing being damaged.

Does this mean that I would prefer soft classical music to be playing in the background in restaurants? Not necessarily. The composer Robert Starer once told his class at Brooklyn College that he had been to a restaurant where classical music was being played. While he was having his soup, he asked management to please turn it off, as it was too much for him. He said that he would have preferred rock, rather than music that requires your full attention.

I have suffered through weddings in which I had to lean on a table with my elbows while pressing the flaps of my ears with my index fingers. Would I be discovered? Did I look foolish?

At venues where I have voiced my displeasure, I have had people tell me, "It's a party! The music is *supposed* to be loud."

I can anticipate the reaction that many readers might have to what I have written: "He's too sensitive," "If he hates noise so much, why doesn't he stay out of restaurants, and/or retire to a desert island, where the sounds of the real world won't be present?"

The above list *does* sound like a whole laundry list of complaints. But it is precisely *because* I love beautiful sounds and music so much — at appropriate times and in appropriate venues — that I hate noise for noise's sake. When I hear a great musical masterpiece or the sound of a singer with a miraculous voice, I appreciate it even more.

This is analogous to some of the self-help gurus who preach that we should love *everyone*. If we do not discriminate, and love a scoundrel as much as we love a saint, what does this say about the love we feel for the saint (who has *earned* that love through his actions? To love someone undeserving of love cheapens the entire concept of what love should represent.

CHAPTER 22

Music As Manipulation

I have been reciting the phrase "Music begins where words end," before I read that Aaron Copland had said this.[40] I really believe it, though. The animal kingdom communicates with one another, and even though we don't understand all of their "languages," actions, and sounds, we know that they have meanings. Man invented spoken language — including subsections, such as sign language — to communicate. Spoken language is probably the most prevalent form, although many other forms of communication are used. Spoken communication enables us to function more efficiently in society, and to convey our needs. But there are a plethora of visual, tactile, and verbal stimuli (not involving words) in the lexicon of communication. Perhaps the most beautiful and intimate is music.[41]

Our facial expressions, mannerisms, and body language are like a language all their own. We all know that a facial expression often needs no translation. Indeed, experts on body language can determine whether someone is lying or not with a high degree of accuracy. Art, written symbols, and the written word are forms of communication. Experts in handwriting analysis can determine characteristics of a person through their writing strokes.

But with music, a composer really "strips himself naked," (another oft-repeated, but true cliché) through sound. Because sounds convey emotions that lie between the lines, a person in a foreign country — who does not understand a particular spoken language — can understand the feelings and emotions conveyed in a piece of music.

All of us have different backgrounds, contexts, imagine different visual images, and feel different emotions while listening to the same music. Unless it is *program music*, where the piece was written to depict something specific, one person's interpretation is no more "authentic," "accurate," or "valid" than another's. The very fact that the same piece of music says different things to different people is all part of its beauty and mystery. This is why composers — even when asked what their piece was meant to convey — often decline to offer an "answer"...preferring the listener to discover his *own* meaning.

Music is a miracle; we need it. It uplifts us, inspires us, cheers us up when we are down, makes us cry with its great beauty and majesty, and with the stirring emotions it conveys. It also brings people together, as when they go to concerts to experience a bonding through a common love. Our differences become less significant than our similarities.

We love to listen to a particular song, because it reminds us of the lover we were with when we first heard it. Music is an omnipresent addition to lovemaking, as are flowers, cologne, perfume, incense, and lingerie. But there are some realms where I feel that music, however beautiful, is an encumbrance.

Music is played in the background in films. Composers watch the films, compose the music, and the music is inserted in appropriate places. Music in the opening introduction of a movie can be effective, if a sexy song correlates to the frame of mind the movie wants to convey. A James Bond film, for example, conveys a macho image, danger, intrigue, high living, elegance, beautiful women, and sex.

But in the midst of a stirring virtuoso performance — where the characterization and acting is the raison d'être, background music is usually an intrusion. I feel the same for documentaries and radio commercials. Our emotions are being manipulated; we are being told what to feel by the music, without being allowed to draw our own conclusions. In *Schindler's List*, the horrors depicted are so heart-wrenching that we don't need to hear John Williams' beautiful and achingly sad theme as an accompaniment. Very often, the music is the difference between whether a person cries or not during a sad movie. The music represents that final yank of our heart strings.

Imagine a movie in which an actor has to portray a character who has gone several days without sleep. One approach might be for him to go without sleep *himself*. He would look and feel like the character he is portraying.

But another school of thought would be to scoff at this approach, and consider it to be "taking the easy way out." Proponents of this school would argue that as an actor, one should not have to *resort* to this. He should be able to achieve an accurate portrayal and *become* the character through the power of his acting skill.[42]

This is how I feel about a film trying to convey deep, emotional, and complex characterization. Don't take the easy way out by "telling" the viewer what to feel. There is no music playing in the background in everyday life situations, to complement or augment the intensity of arguments, couples deciding upon divorce, people hearing about tragedies, etc.

As for the ad for hospice treatment from Calgary Hospital that I hear on the radio...I'm sure they are a compassionate and caring hospital, and are providing an important service. But *please*...cut the sad music as the woman is describing the care and treatment her father was given during his final days. It is manipulative, and smacks of commercialism. Of course, the ad *is* a commercial, and is run for the purposes of having people choose Calgary for their loved ones. Everyone needs money to live. But with music playing in the background, it makes the ad more "commercial" than it has to be.

When watching YouTube videos of female bodybuilders, a wide array of music can be chosen…whether they are doing a posing routine, or whether it is merely a woman working out at the gym. The music is presumably chosen to complement the video. Often, the videos are accompanied by heavy metal "music," which a guy is screaming to. It is so excruciating to listen to, that I have to immediately turn the sound off. It is almost *physically* painful.

But our own likes and dislikes are what make people different. Who am I to tell someone that what they like is offering an inferior experience? He may feel the same way about Bach and Chopin. I have the freedom not to listen to this music, or to avoid the concerts where this music is being performed. If I don't like a certain art exhibit, I don't have to see it. If I don't like a radio show or a particular host, I can turn it off, or not tune in.

We don't *have* to like everything someone else does, or agree with everything someone else believes. Even lovers will not agree on everything, nor have identical interests. But wouldn't that be too boring if they did? Does anyone want a clone? What *is* necessary in an "ideal" partnership is the sharing of *core* values. Part of the mystery and pleasure of being in love is to learn about — or at least be exposed to — your partner's interests, to explore, to grow, and to evolve. In love, as in life, that's what it's all about.

Notes

1. Chapter 1, page 5: I got the idea for this statement from Nathaniel Branden. *In Judgment Day: My Years With Ayn Rand* (page 26), he writes, "I had a sudden sense of the universe as a total, and I thought: if God is needed to explain the existence of the universe, then what explains the existence of God? If God does exist, he's at least as marvelous and impressive as the universe — and no less in need of an explanation. But then who created whatever created God?" I would have preferred that the last sentence didn't have the word "whatever created" in it. But Branden was evidently making the point, that if something created God, then something would have had to create whatever *created* God ad infinitum.

2. Chapter 1, page 7: It was pointed out to me that the definition of "fear" in "God-fearing" is an archaic usage that is more akin to "respect." *Random House Webster's College Dictionary* defines God-fearing as: 1. "deeply respectful or fearful of God." 2. (*sometimes l.c.*) deeply religious; pious; devout. [1825-35]

   The above statement might be accurate, but is it not often implied that when a person does not adhere to the rites and rituals inherent in their religion that they will be punished with a sin?

3. Chapter 1, page 12: This statement was not my original idea, but came from what Bob Costas said in his June 1992 *Playboy* interview.

4. Chapter 1, page 13: In an interview, when asked if he believed in God, pianist Arthur Rubinstein said that he didn't believe in a gentleman with a beard.

5. Chapter 3, page 26: Let me be clear; I am not advocating the wanton hunting and killing of Nazis. I might *celebrate* their destruction, but would not personally kill them unless it was in self-defense. Everyone has a right to think their own thoughts, however vile, as long as they don't act upon them. If a Nazi is caught in the act of trying to harm or kill people, they should be responded to with deadly force. But I personally would not respond in this manner to the woman at the gas station. If I were caught, I would be allowing my hatred of her to *victimize* me, not just *offend* me, as I would go to prison for a long time.

6. Chapter 3, page 27: To those who would criticize burning a child molester's house down, I would ask them what the difference is between that, and the target assassinations of Palestinian terrorists by the Israelis. What is the difference between that, and the bombing of the homes of suicide bombers? What is the difference between that, and the employment of a hit squad to take out Osama bin Laden?

7. Chapter 3, page 28: A phrase psychologist Nathaniel Branden has used.

8. Chapter 6, page 50: I once visited my cousin in Los Angeles, and she lent me her car for the evening. When I wanted to return, I mistakenly went into two separate cars, respectively, which looked identical to hers. Both had been left unlocked. Even inside one of them, I was not entirely sure it was not my cousin's car...so I opened the glove compartment. Had I been caught by the owners, they would not have believed that I had innocently entered the cars with absolutely no intent to steal them or any of their contents. The police or anyone else would not have believed me, either.

9. Chapter 6, page 50: A similar case involved someone who stole

a bicycle.

10. Chapter 6, page 51: Someone might ask why the homeowner didn't install video surveillance. First of all, an owner has a right to install or not to install anything that he wishes on *his* property. For a criminal to make a claim against the homeowner for wounding him, is like someone making claims against the owners of a junk yard they broke into, for being attacked by the guard dogs. Sometimes, it is posted that a place is under video surveillance, sometimes not. Again, that is the prerogative of the owner. It might be argued that it is better *not* to make any claims of security. If a criminal is warned beforehand, this gives him the advantage of preparing his circumvention. The wearing of masks is one such countermove; the use of gloves to avoid leaving fingerprints increases the criminal's odds of not getting caught, whether or not the premises are under video surveillance.

11. Chapter 7, page 56: I am *not* impressed by the people who have "found Jesus" after their crimes were committed. Why don't they ever find Him *before*?

12. Chapter 7, page 57: Many years ago, G. Gordon Liddy was a guest on *The Dick Cavett Show*. The discussion was about killing someone for preventive as opposed to retributive reasons. Liddy objected to the word "murder," that Cavett kept using, because it was opposite to what he considered it to be. The very fact that the word "murder," as opposed to "kill," was being used, implied unjustified killing by definition. Liddy kept arguing his point, but Cavett kept insisting on using the word "murder."

During the course of the conversation, Cavett reached up to swat a fly (or pretended to do so). He told Liddy that he had just killed a fly, and asked whether this posed any moral problems for him. With a deliciously pleasant insouciance, Liddy replied,

"No, I admire your skill." I cherished the exchange, and wished I had been the recipient of the compliment.

13. Chapter 9, page 67: Quote taken from Wikipedia, the free encyclopedia.

14. Chapter 9, page 67: Ibid.

15. Chapter 10, page 79: from *Norman Sandler: Kenpo Stylist*, by Richard Devens, *WUSHU KUNG FU*, Fall 1993

16. Chapter 12, page 100: Eubie Blake, who smoked cigarettes and lived to 100, said that if he had known he would live so long, he would have taken better care of himself.

17. Chapter 13, page 106: It might be argued that comparing harmful foods to PEDs is irrelevant to this discussion, because the issue is "performance enhancement." The former does not enhance performance, but the latter has been proven to do so.

    But when examined in the context of a person's sovereignty over his body (and therefore his right to put into it anything he wants), a discussion relating harmful foods to PEDs *is* relevant. The former might not be illegal (and might not have given an athlete an "unfair advantage"), but I am suggesting in this chapter that harmful foods or additives (such as aspartame) might be just as harmful as PEDs.

    The inclusion of vitamins—which people *supplement* with—*can* be compared to PEDs, because although the former is contained in foods, it is technically *not* a food, but an organic compound.

18. Chapter 15, page 117: I once witnessed a chicken about to get his neck slit, and knew beyond a doubt, from the furious screeches it emitted, that this chicken knew what was in store for him.

19. Chapter 16, page 123: I have no intention of offending the many beautiful homosexual people whose love for each other can certainly be as genuine and passionate as the love between a man and a woman. I am heterosexual, so I choose to write within my own personal context. This in no way implies, when I write about man/woman love, that the material is not applicable to man/man or woman/woman love.

20. Chapter 16, page 125: "I have often "fallen in love" with women I have seen on the street, in the subway, in clubs, restaurants, on the beach, etc. (usually without hearing their voices). When I *did* hear a woman's voice, it almost always corresponded to her physical appearance. This does not mean I knew what her voice would sound like. It meant that when I loved a woman's looks, I usually loved her voice. You may not yet "know" a woman, but based on physical attraction, you know right away who you are *not* attracted to, and who you are wildly sexually attracted to.

    Many years ago, I met an extremely beautiful woman on a blind date, who told me there was no "chemistry." I mentioned to my mother that I had met a fabulous woman who didn't want *me.* "You're looking too high," she said. What does this say about her opinion of *me?* She suggested I get someone *dumpy.* When I indicated that that was not the kind of woman I had in mind, she said, "Go ahead; keep waiting. You'll never get anybody." I don't wish to *keep waiting,* but I'd rather wait and find the right one — and have the feeling be reciprocal — than to settle for anyone just because I'm "running out of time."

21. Chapter 16, page 128: This reminds me of something I see in the *personals* all the time. A female poster will write: "No phonies, jerks, or assholes need respond." Reading this shit, I can't help imagining a scenario of a man reading the posting, and liking what he reads, until he gets to the ending. He says to himself,

"Gee, I would have wanted to respond, but I happen to be an ass-hole, so I'd better not." I've seen a lot of assholes in my lifetime, but I've never encountered a person who *knew* he was one.

I've even seen ads where women write, "If you're not an honest person, don't respond" (which is even more stupid, if that is possible). Are they asking a man to be honest about his dishonesty?

22. Chapter 16, page 128: Artificial insemination required a seminal ejaculation at a prior time.

23. Chapter 16, page 130: I acknowledge that there are male pros-titutes and gigolos, but in our society, the practice of a woman paying a man for sex hasn't caught on on a widespread basis. There are a plethora of homosexual prostitutes, but I wish to confine myself to female prostitutes for the purpose of this topic.

24. Chapter 16, page 132: In *Everything You Always Wanted To Know About Sex: But Were Afraid To Ask*, Dr. David Reuben wrote that most prostitutes are lesbians, and hate men.

25. Chapter 16, page 133: I refer to those who would *like* to experi-ence sex, not to those who have no desire to have it. Sometimes, a person's religion forbids him to have it, and a priest may not want it for this reason...although some desire it anyway.

26. Chapter 16, page 137: In some states, same-sex marriage is now legal. I only refer to marriage as a union between a man and a woman for purposes of this book.

27. Chapter 16, page 138: Or by the desire to properly follow their religion.

28. Chapter 16, page 139: I know someone whose sister married a gay man so that she could get a green card and become a US citizen.

It worked out very well for both of them, and the woman's family loves him like a son.

29. Chapter 16, page 140: He might not even *think* his wife is deficient, and might even have a wonderful marriage *and* sex life. Sometimes, an affair can make a man or woman discover just how superior his or her spouse is to the people they are having an affair with, and also make them realize why the possible jeopardization of the marriage for a lesser value would be foolish.

   Religious people might consider adultery wrong under any circumstances, but since I am an atheist, I write without a religious frame of reference.

30. Chapter 16, page 140: This topic brings to mind the Rev. Dr. Martin Luther King, Jr. and the Rev. Jesse Jackson, both of whom had extramarital affairs.

31. Chapter 16, page 142: There are procedures that can make a person taller, but are extreme measures that are not common in this country. I trust that the reader understands what I am talking about.

32. Chapter 17, page 146: I will never forget the headline of the sports pages of *The New York Post* on the eve of Muhammad Ali's fight with George Foreman (October 30, 1974) in Kinshasa, Zaire (the *Democratic Republic of the Congo*, since 1997) for the heavyweight championship of the world (The Rumble in the Jungle). Boxing "expert" Lester Bromberg (1909–1989), wrote *Ali Has No Chance.*

33. Chapter 17 page 147: This example of a logical impossibility was used by Chaim Potok in one of his books (not reproduced verbatim). A child is having a conversation with someone, and he is asking questions about God.

34. Chapter 17 page 148: I decided to make *TRUE LIES AND HIDDEN MEANINGS* a subsection of *THE THINGS WE SAY*. Unlike some of the statements that people make that I list in the latter (which people actually *believe*), the former is a collection of lines that people use to get out of situations more easily. They are so prevalent that they have become an accepted form of lying. I borrowed the heading from the 1994 movie starring Arnold Schwarzenegger, and translate their meanings.

35. Chapter 17, page 148: In *ACTION! Nothing Happens Until Something Moves*, Robert Ringer talks about what people really mean when they tell you they are "super busy." When I dug up an article I had written many years ago to use in this book, it was remarkable how similar our words were. But I wrote them before I ever read Ringer's book.

36. Chapter 17, page 153: "I'm hangin' in there" is one of the most common "answers" to the question, "How are you?" Similarly, it answers the question, while saying and revealing nothing. Its equivalent, in the personal ad headings of female posters is, "Looking for Mr. Right."

37. Chapter 19, page 180: This is one of the reasons why I find the concept of praying to a "supreme being" so repulsive. If there *is* a supreme being, He became one (if He wasn't "created") by "accident" (chance); and *if* His existence is by "accident," He would have come *into* existence in the same manner that *I* did. We both would have had no say in our respective "creations" (births).

For those who would say I am pretending to know the unknowable, by calling His existence an "accident" (assuming He *does* exist), I would counter that *they* are attempting to assert the unknowable as truth (when it cannot be knowable). They are taking the easy way out, because if it is asserted that He always existed, then they automatically win all arguments via no logic. When that fails, nonbelievers or agnostics are asked to put the cart before the horse and have *faith*. *Then* we will "see" what we want to see.

With all of the great advances in the sciences, including astronomy and physics, we know but a tiny fraction of all there is to know about the size and origin of the universe. Man has physically made it only to the moon, so far. But there are planets and space extending millions of light years into infinity. There may be an end to it, but the distance is so vast, that man will never find out a fraction of the answers. Our lifetimes are but a microscopic blip in time. Yet the men of God can assert with "certainty" that God always existed. Maybe they are right, and I am wrong. But until they prove it, I won't let them force me to ignore all the *non-evidence* of my senses; I won't succumb to their trick of demanding that I explain why I don't believe in something that *they* cannot prove; I won't allow them to cause me to surrender my mind to believe in, and to know, the unknowable.

38. Chapter 19, page 181: One time, a person who did not need my services called me back to tell me he got my message, didn't need anyone at the moment, but would keep my information on file. I really appreciated it, because this almost never happens.

39. Chapter 19, page 182: Isn't it ironic? I would often allow a telemarketer to keep me on the phone, and they would end up hanging up abruptly on *me* once they realized they weren't going to get anything.

40. Chapter 22, page 199: Whether or not he was the first, I don't know.

41. Chapter 22, page 199: Aaron Copland has also said that if you

want to know him, listen to his music.

42. Chapter 22, page 201: It has been said that Laurence Olivier conveyed this thought to Dustin Hofmann during the filming of *Marathon Man* (1976). The accounts of the exchange, however (by third parties and by Hoffmann himself), vary as to what actually happened, and what was said and/or meant.